Dixie Dateline

New Series, No. 1

DIXIE
DATELINE

A Journalistic Portrait of the Contemporary South

Edited and with an Introduction
by John B. Boles

Rice University Studies

Houston, Texas

Contents

Introduction
The Dixie Difference

JOHN B. BOLES

Any prospective reader of a book of essays on the modern South might expect a certain consensus of viewpoints, a commonly accepted definition of the region, even a general agreement about the South's past, if not its future. But such is not the case with the eleven essays by eminent journalists collected here. No single conclusion, no mutually accepted point of view emerges. What the South is, whether it is persisting as a distinct region or vanishing into a great homogenous American culture, or whether that "loss" should be applauded, regretted, or prevented by some intellectual cardiopulmonary contraption, remains a riddle that different individuals answer differently. It has always been so with the South. Everyone has a ready image of the region, but the closer one comes to examine the South, the more the differences merge into similarities, and vice versa. Like a giant sphinx on the American land—as one historian called it—Dixie beckons investigators even as it resists explication. Therein of course lies its attraction.

The South is both American and something different, at times a mirror or magnifier of national traits and at other times a counterculture. That difference has been good, bad, and indefinable, but it has long been felt. The eleven explorers of the region's society and psyche represented here do not finally solve the enigma, but they bring fresh intelligence to bear on

old questions and open up new vistas for understanding the most provocative and mysterious section of America. After a generation of unprecedented change, after a southern president, after a flurry of scholarship, the
South still challenges those who try to separate image from reality, stereotype from myth. Accepting the difficulty of consensus, wary of simple
truths, adventurous readers will find here hard thinking, suggestive analysis, but ultimately no single key to understanding the South. And that
makes the whole endeavor not futile but exciting. The southern character
is too complex for easy answers, and southerners—at least the publishing
kind—enjoy the perennial search for southern identity.

For at least two centuries Americans have recognized a distinctive
South, and perhaps there is no more enduring regional image in the
American mind than that of a Dixie different from the rest of the nation. In
a famous letter to the Marquis de Chastellux, dated September 2, 1785,
Thomas Jefferson compared the characteristics of northerners and south-
erners by listing their traits in parallel columns:

In the North they are	In the South they are
cool	fiery
sober	voluptuary
laborious	indolent
persevering	unsteady
independant [*sic*]	independant [*sic*]
jealous of their own liber- ties, and just to those of others	zealous for their own liber- ties, but trampling on those of others
interested	generous
chicaning	candid
superstitious and hypocriti- cal in their religion	without attachment or pre- tensions to any religion but that of the heart

Jefferson was so certain that these traits conformed to geographical setting
that he wrote: "An observing traveller, without aid of the quadrant, may
always know his latitude by the character of the people among whom he
finds himself."

Jefferson ascribed the South's peculiarities to "that warmth of their climate," a judgment echoed almost a century and a half later by U. B. Phillips of Yale University. Georgia-born Phillips, the first great southern historian, commenced his classic account of the Old South with the sentence, "Let us begin by discussing the weather, for that has been the chief agency in making the South distinctive." We are less concerned here with the role of climate or the accuracy of Jefferson's classification than with the underlying assumption of southern distinctiveness. That idea grew slowly. Historians still debate when the South emerged as a self-consciously separate section, perceived as such also by the nation as a whole. Taking their cue from Jefferson and pronouncements made by delegates from several southern states during and shortly after the chaos of the American Revolution, some historians argue that the "South"—as distinct from the geographically southern colonies—existed as early as 1776, set apart even then by slavery.

Historians of course are no more likely to agree than are economists or theologians. Few scholars accept this early a date for the existence of full-blown southern identity. Instead, most view the long generation following the Treaty of Paris (1783) as the high-water-mark of southern Americanism, when southerners were at the liberal forefront of national decisionmaking and in fact controlled four of the first five presidential administrations. Washington, Jefferson, Madison, and Monroe were nation-builders, not dismantlers of the Union. For many twentieth-century southern liberals, these founding fathers represented the true South, the Great South, before slavery interests and John C. Calhoun led the region down the seductive path of sectionalism, then secession, Civil War, and Reconstruction, to sharecropping and colonial status within the nation.

There is a pleasing symmetry to this view, for it allows one to think of the history of southernness as a kind of long aberration, ended perhaps in 1976 when southerner Jimmy Carter became president. The great break occurred sometime between the War of 1812—when even John C. Calhoun was a fiercely nationalistic "war hawk"—and the early 1830s, by which time the nullification crisis in the South and the rise of modern antislavery activities in the North called forth a militant southern sectionalism. Perhaps the pivotal year was 1819, when the debate over the admission of Missouri as a state raised the critical question of the expansion of slavery. In that year also the deep economic depression—the Panic of 1819—highlighted profound economic differences between North and South. In retrospect it seems that a southern recognition of divergent values, contrasting social and economic systems, and an emerging distinctive culture began that eventful year, a full century and a half after the slavery-plantation system had developed.

Once the perception arose that the South had a unique destiny, events were interpreted to prove the perception. Old realities were observed in a new light. Many contemporaries saw the divisive issues and dilemmas of the next four decades as springing from the essential dichotomy between North and South. From this perspective the Civil War became necessary, even irrepressible, for a southern nation had arisen with manifold interests so different that continued union was impossible. Thus the Civil War, the apex of southern separateness, appears almost predetermined, with the long and often arduous century afterwards being merely the slow process by which the South was brought back into the Union, first legally in 1876, then politically in 1976, and not quite yet economically.

In this sense of the South's finally rejoining the nation, some commentators heralded Jimmy Carter's election to the presidency as ending the region's long sojourn as a separate province. How appropriate it seemed, on the nation's 200th birthday, for the great sectional rapprochement to occur. Yet those who thought that the nation was finally done with things distinctly southern were ill-prepared for the next few years. Punsters quickly labeled the Carter-Mondale team "Grits and Fritz," and Jimmy's brother Billy added a new dimension to the stereotype of the Good Ole Boy. With toe-tapping country music in the White House and recipes for catfish in the *New York Times*, southern fried chic seemed to suit the national taste. The subtitle of John Egerton's book, *The Southernization of America*, was perhaps more appropriate than its title, *The Americanization of Dixie*. The upshot of the matter was the question, with the South becoming more like the North, or vice versa, was there validity any more to the hoary concept of the distinctive South? Journalists vied with sociologists and historians to describe the death of Dixie. Their efforts proved premature.

Of course even an attempt to eulogize the South implies the assumption of regional distinctiveness, and the origin of that assumption lies intertwined with much of American history. For two centuries Americans North and South have felt a need to define the Dixie difference. In the antebellum days of slavery and plantations the South's economy and its labor system differentiated it from the rest of the nation, but southerners, feeling defensive about their peculiar institution and not a little guilty, sought to apotheosize their society. Real regional differences were exaggerated and elaborated upon. Like whistling in the dark to dispel fears and doubts, southerners tried, largely successfully, to persuade themselves that theirs was a higher form of civilization than the frenzied, industrial North. According to the plantation legend, the South produced gentlemen rather than vulgar businessmen; a leisurely life of manners and lofty thoughts rather than a hurried, pell-mell struggle for ever-higher profits; a working class of contented slaves, not sullen, unruly factory laborers. Thus the myth of the Old South emerged, but not entirely because it soothed southern consciences. Many northern intellectuals, dismayed by the social changes being wrought by the incipient Industrial Revolution, helped create the plantation legend and then used it to criticize the changing North. The Old South of moonlight and magnolias, of carefree hospitality and happy-go-lucky Sambos, served both regions as myths usually do, relieving social tensions and reconciling conflicting values.

During the generation before the Civil War both North and South conspired to create an image of the South, an illusion that never bore close resemblance to reality. For their contrasting needs Americans in the two regions constructed self-serving portraits of the Old South, an exotic, romantic "touched-up" portrait with the diversity, the conflict, the frontier aspects of the South removed. In the aftermath of Appomattox, white southerners, suffering a depression of both morale and money, sought to recoup some of their pride by romanticizing the Old South with a vengeance, constructing a never-never land of moss, magnolias, mansions, and mammies. Many southern clergy found meaning in Confederate defeat by arguing that God was thereby testing the South for a higher purpose, the reformation of the nation along the lines of evangelical Protestantism. Southern traditions were united with biblical themes to produce a religion of the Lost Cause, a faith that practically equated the heritage of Dixie with Holy Scripture.

Following Reconstruction, secular advocates of an urban, industrial "New South" of profits and progress helped sell their program, legitimate themselves as southern, and assuage vague guilt feelings about imitating the Yankees by piously glorifying the Old South. Joel Chandler Harris, for example, wrote booster editorials by day and Uncle Remus stories by night, seemingly without noticing the conflict. Ever since, students have labored under the heavy burden of myth and contradiction. In fact, much historical scholarship in the twentieth century has been an attempt to de-mythologize the popular notions of southern history. The list of myths de-bunked is long—the Lazy South, the Romantic South, the Cavalier South, the New South. Historians point out again and again, for example, that the large majority of southern whites in 1860 did not own slaves; that Re-construction was not a "blackout of honest government"; that slaves were not happy Sambos; that Sunbelt notions to the contrary, the South is still the nation's poorest region. But the myths live on. Now historians are turning their attention to the function of myths, how they have helped shape southern history by forging unity, offering rationales for action, providing a common goal.

After acknowledging the prevalence of several mythical Souths and then trying to analyze the reality behind the facade, one quickly realizes that more riddles abound. Even defining the South quickly transcends geography to become a problem in cultural and intellectual history. Simple geography brings difficulties. The Mason-Dixon Line does not suffice as a boundary between North and South, for such a division would assign Del-aware to the South. If we were to consider the former Confederate states as delimiting the South, we would be excluding Maryland and Kentucky, two important slave states, as well as Missouri. Some expansive Sunbelt the-oreticians would lump the Southeast along with New Mexico, Arizona, and much of California and call the broad swath of geography "the south-ern rim," meanwhile searching in vain for parallels between southern Cal-ifornia and South Carolina. In this century migrations of southerners northward and northerners southward have blurred the boundaries. Much of southern Illinois and Indiana have a southern cast, as do sections of Detroit; and Bakersfield, California, is a southern enclave in the West. The Virginia suburbs of Washington, D. C., the coastal areas of the Florida peninsula, and the cosmopolitan suburbs of Houston and Atlanta have been so penetrated by persons of northern birth as to lead to a proliferation of delicatessens and the easy availability—even home delivery—of the *New York Times*. Where does the South begin and end?

To make matters worse, any geographical concept of the South conveys the false impression of homogeneity. Expressions such as "the Solid South" have created the image of a monolithic region, a huge, warm, culturally flat region of slow-talking people who prefer grits with breakfast and their pork barbecued. Yet within the South there is variety of every kind: geological, climatic, cultural, ethnic. Even the favored styles of barbecue differ. The piedmont and mountain areas of Virginia, North Carolina, and Tennessee are as different from the coastal plains of Louisiana as Savannah is from Dallas. The Texas Germans and Czechs, the Louisiana Cajuns, and the North Carolina Moravians are people very different from the First Families of Virginia (the FFVs) and the aristocracies of Charleston and New Orleans. The mountain folk of the Appalachian valleys share little with Texas wildcatters or Georgia blacks. Yet all are southerners. One of the important roles of myth has been to create an illusion of unity out of this diversity. Similarly, students of the region, seeking to impose order on a crazy-quilt topic, have labored mightily to find a central theme of southern history with which to comprehend the whole. In many ways the search for a central theme has been the central theme of southern history; that quest now has added urgency because of the perception that the South is slowly, before our very eyes, disappearing as a definable entity.

Despite the historical uses and convenience of myths and stereotypes in characterizing or describing the region, most students of the South accept the truth that there really is something different about Dixie. From Jefferson's day the climate has frequently been interpreted as having played a major role in making the South distinctive. According to this view, a long growing season allowed the South to satisfy world demand for tobacco and cotton. The successful introduction of these crops led in turn to the rise of the broad-acred plantation system with its need for cheap labor, a need ultimately met by Negro slavery. Here then were the essential ingredients of southern history: a rural, agricultural region dominated by large planters, with a suppressed racial minority on the bottom. In tangible, measurable ways, the antebellum South was different from the antebellum North. From this fact emerged images of the romantic Old South, as well as the idea, expressed best in 1928 by U. B. Phillips, that the essence of southernism was "a common resolve indomitably maintained" that the South "shall be and remain a white man's country." Whether "expressed with the frenzy of a demagogue or maintained with a patrician's quietude," this was, according to Phillips, "the cardinal test of a Southerner and the central theme of Southern history." The myth of a planter aristocracy, the theme of an agrarian republic, the identification of the South with gracious living or white domination or rural-dominated Bible-Belt religion or one-party politics—all have evolved from the old assumption that environment shaped events.

The economy and society that were made possible and produced by the climate gave rise to a people who possessed certain characteristics, and many observers have shifted their attention away from the immediate consequences of climate and focused on those acquired human traits that seem to define southerners. Rather than its crops, it is its people and their character that distinguish the region. Because geography fails, we turn to defining the South as a region possessing a unique folk culture, or having experienced a history very unlike the rest of the nation. The South becomes a way of living, a sense of belonging, a state of mind. W. J. Cash's great book, *The Mind of the South*, is the classic of this genre, although in his emphasis on southerners' feeling instead of thinking, on their simple hedonism mixed with a rigid Puritanical streak, Cash came close to arguing that the South did not have a mind. Southerners, it seems, *are* more violent, more religious, more conservative, more fatalistic than nonsoutherners. Thinking does affect behavior. Statistics show that the southern death rate from tornadoes, for example, is significantly higher than elsewhere, and the best explanation is that southerners ignore warnings and neglect to build storm cellars in the belief that if your time has come, you can't escape, and if your time has not come, then why bother with precaution. Southerners also speak differently, whether with a Georgia drawl or an East Texas twang, and have an infatuation with words, a tendency to express themselves not in straightforward analytical prose but with detailed, richly textured stories. Roy Reed's essay exemplifies this folk attribute. The love affair with talk may explain the world-renowned outpouring of southern fiction, as well as the disproportionate number and influence of southern journalists and historians—people who, after all, mainly tell stories. Even that most southern of music, labeled "country," is peculiarly concerned with the stories that unfold in the lyrics.

In recent decades the quest to understand southern distinctiveness has produced more emphasis on the human dimension. David Potter, a Georgia-born historian who taught at Rice, Yale, and Stanford universities, argued that southern identity inhered in what he called a unique folk culture. In this folk society a sense of belonging, a relatedness of people to people and people to land, persisted amidst a national culture that was increasingly urban and technological. This identification with place and family seemed to be particularly true among rural southerners, and the South remained largely rural until after World War II. The urban areas in the South today are still peopled mostly by rural folk who have migrated to the cities in search of jobs. They have brought with them their tastes in food, music, sports, and religion. In subtle ways they have changed the cities, and certainly their urban residence has changed their expectations, even if it has not rendered them completely urbane. During the decade of the 1970s, Dixie was the only region of the nation in which urban growth outpaced rural growth. The rising generation of city-born southerners will determine whether the South can survive urbanization and remain recognizably southern. If southernness is merely an artifact of rurality, then it will soon be gone with the winds of change and growth. Sociological data shows, however, that educated, urban southerners continue to attend church far more regularly than their counterparts nationally and identify themselves with their homeplaces with greater intensity than northerners—an indication that southern values will persist in the cities.

Realizing that the bulldozer revolution of urban sprawl and industrialization would eventually end the South's rural isolation, and that the Supreme Court's desegregation decision in *Brown* v. *Board of Education of Topeka* in 1954 would ultimately end the white South's intransigence on race, C. Vann Woodward sought the essence of southernness in the region's peculiar historical experience. According to Woodward, what had made the South different was not its relative absence of cities, its agrarian traditions, its inordinate concern with race, or its political practices, but rather the way it had been treated by time itself.

Writing a generation ago, Woodward contrasted the nation's history of prosperity—being the people of plenty—with the South's long travail of poverty, stretching from the rise of sharecropping to the trough of the Great Depression, when President Franklin D. Roosevelt called the region the nation's number one economic problem. Moreover, although no nation in all history had succeeded like the United States, winning all its wars and spreading its banner from sea to shining sea, the South had failed, and failed utterly, in its one great attempt to have a separate national destiny. And while the nation—born in liberty, protector of the Union, and emancipator of the slaves—basked in innocence, the South had to live with the guilt of slavery and secession bearing heavily on its soul. Thus, Woodward concluded, in a nation marked by success, prosperity, and innocence, the South was set apart by its failure, poverty, and guilt. That collective experience, shared by all southerners, gave them a sense of identity, a common heritage apart from the national norm. The South's history, a past that was not dead, defined the southern character. A sense of tragedy, a recognition of frailty and limits to endeavor marked the regional psyche. Because the southern experience has been more akin to the world experience than the northern experience has been, southern literature both fictional and historical attracts an enormous audience abroad. Moreover, two quintessential southern musical forms, jazz and country, enjoy a global acceptance. The southern encounter with history has ironically produced an intensely localistic people with universal dilemmas and international appeal.

Of course, in the years since Woodward made his influential analysis, the nation has undergone a series of shocks. In the aftermath of Vietnam, Watergate, and the discovery of poverty in the land of plenty—what

Michael Harrington called "The Other America"—the national experience no longer seems so different from that of the South. And with the South solving its racial problems arguably more satisfactorily than the North, with Sunbelt prosperity narrowing the regional income gap, and with a recent southern president, one might even argue that the regions have flip-flopped. Such of course is not the case, but southerners now feel much freer of that scorn once directed their way, and are finding "Snowbelt" envy much more gratifying.

The southern folk culture that has experienced a history unlike the rest of the United States is in many ways biracial. In the South blacks and whites have lived together, cheek by jowl, for more than three hundred years. Nothing and no one in the South has escaped the mutual influences of the two races. Black values and styles have helped shape the white culture, and vice versa, to such an extent that today it is impossible to separate the strands. Southerners are truly both the white and black inhabitants of the region. Hearing Elvis Presley borrow from black vocal traditions or Charlie Pride singing Hank Williams, or eating southern home cooking, or listening to southern preachers or gospel singers, who can deny that we truly are one at the same time that we are two people?

But the question remains: where is and what is the South today? Efforts to reappraise the South seem to proliferate shortly after every period of change. At the end of the 1950s, Arkansas journalist Harry Ashmore wrote a perceptive book entitled *An Epitaph for Dixie*, but historian Francis B. Simkins of Virginia countered with *The Everlasting South*. Parallel titles could be supplied down to the present, with concern ever being raised about *The Americanization of Dixie*, then laid aside with reflections on *The Enduring South*. As change erodes the characteristics that were once thought to define the South—poverty, rurality, educational and "cultural" backwardness, segregation, Democratic hegemony—the South's separate existence seems threatened. With that threat of loss, writers of every sort start examining the region, hunting for surviving fossils of the past or subtle new forms of southern identity, and lo, that very concern with self-identity betrays a very southern habit of wanting to know who you are and from whence you came. That concern with family, with place, with "relatedness" that so epitomizes the southerner produces a spate of regional analysis and nostalgia and, yes, even pious self-congratulation that keeps the South alive. Whether one assumes that there is still a tangible essence that sets the region apart or that one must, in the face of modernization and homogenization, "Dixiefy Dixie" (as Edwin Yoder puts it) to keep the image alive artificially, the search for southern identity has continued for at least two centuries and shows no signs of faltering or concluding.

With the South, as with much else, a great deal lies in the eye of the beholder. High technology, interstate highways, and industrial growth may threaten one vision of the South, but recorded country music, fast food outlets for fried chicken and biscuits and sausage, C-B radios in eighteen-wheelers crackling with good-ole-boy talk from their drivers, and the working poor who have moved from the fields to the factories keep alive memories of the past. Southern speech patterns and that signal form of ethnic identification, gastronomic preferences, show sure signs of resisting change. While the architecture and form of southern cities appear as standardized as American cities elsewhere, as Neal R. Peirce convincingly demonstrates, in human terms the texture of life in them reveals surprising continuity with the rural past. Yet popular images often lag behind changing reality, and the myth of southern distinctiveness may ultimately be more tenacious, and more significant, than actuality. Perceptive journalists such as John A. Crowl can document that southern universities are more than holding their own and subscribing to national standards for research, tenure, and curricula. Yet a "manual" like *The Insiders' Guide to the Colleges* (1971) stereotypically includes most southern universities under the category "Hard Playin', Hard Drinkin', Hard Lovin' Southern Schools." How do myth, perception, and reality merge in the popular mind? The acceptance of diversity, real or imagined, can make a real difference. As long as southerners believe in, fear, or desire a regional identity, or worry about whether one exists, there will be a South. What that South is, precisely speaking, no one can say.

And surely few will not admit that the loss of many "southern characteristics" is a great blessing. The South's long heritage of spirit-breaking poverty, of ignorance and religious prejudice, of savage racism and brutal violence, of irrelevant politics and undemocratic control, took a heavy toll on all southerners. To the extent that *that* South has died, humanity has triumphed. Better schools and improved job opportunities have freed thousands from poverty and given them immeasurably better lives. While city dwellers acknowledge a twinge of nostalgia for life back on the farm, the higher pay, greater scope of entertainment, and educational and medical advantages of urban life keep them in town. Even so, many still identify with their rural homeplaces and intend to retire and be buried there. For the huge majority of southerners, black and white, the South today is certainly a much better place to live than it was a generation ago. The beneficial changes in race relations alone represent a fundamental reshaping of the social, cultural, and political landscape, and give promise of improving relations in the future. The tide of black migration has turned back toward the South, and southern blacks are finding new purpose and meaning in their original American homeland. Even today one is surprised, driving into Montgomery from Atlanta, to see overhead the large green interstate sign proclaiming the "Martin Luther King, Jr., Expressway," but what could be a better symbol of the changing South?

In one sense this whole endeavor of defining and making predictions about the continuity of southernness has an abstract, ersatz quality about it. Most southerners take their sense of regional identity for granted even if they cannot articulate its nature. Perhaps one even has to be a southerner to know really what it is. For southerners, after all, grew up with a perception of differentness that had its roots in that long-ago time when slavery gave a concreteness that has since evaporated to the idea of separate cultures. That folk memory of distinction, imbibed with their mothers' milk, predisposes southerners to assume their distinctiveness, even when tangible evidence is wanting. And for generations, except when threatened by or contrasted to outsiders, the search for regional self-identity was what kept novelists and historians and journalists in business; the folk simply were southerners. The magnitude of the change in recent years, however, has brought urgency, a sense of potential loss, not only to aspiring authors but to average persons who can instinctively sense that they are drifting away from their old world. Often loss brings reflection and renewed appreciation, and exactly that seems to be happening with southernness.

People are suddenly eating homestyle cooking and saying "y'all," purposely being southern as a personal statement of identity. People are no longer ashamed to be southerners. A perception that the South might be disappearing in a cultural sense has led to a discovery of its importance in personal and national terms. Ninety years ago the census revealed that the American frontier was closed; three years later a great historian discovered "The Significance of the Frontier." William K. Stevens indicates that something similar might be happening in the South's largest and most rapidly changing city. Houston's phenomenal growth in population and prosperity has changed its motto from the "Magnolia City" to the "Urban West." A new culture is emerging, neither completely southern nor western. But as Houston becomes less like the Texas of old, with its heritage of openness and individuality, native Houstonians (and transplanted rural Texans) eagerly try to recapture that old ethic. Cowboy chic began not as a movie gimmick but as a grassroots attempt to recapture and hold on to a way of life and a mythical identity that was rapidly disappearing. Moreover, the thousands of mobile Americans from California, Michigan, and New York who have moved to Houston—rootless searchers for economic opportunity and advancement—seize upon the cowboy image in an attempt to legitimate their residence and show that they "belong." While the western cowboy seems to have conquered the southern cavalier in Texas, partly because of the more favorable popular associations of the cowpoke with freedom and "good" and partly because the cowpuncher is a more national hero, Houston's cowboy renaissance may suggest the future of southernness.

As the South disappears in demographic, economic, and political terms, there seems to be a corresponding effort to rediscover and revivify at least certain components of the southern way of life. Opinion molders sense the popular concern, and thus symposia, books, clothing, musical fads, and even college curricula—witness the proliferation of "southern institutes" —speak to that concern. In a very real sense, southerners did not exist until about 1819, when they began to perceive themselves as an identifiable group. The underlying socioeconomic factors that gave substance to the perception existed for more than a century before the perception arose. Self-identification as "southern" was the essence of southernness, and that perception has acquired a life of its own, in large part independent of material reality. Southernness is now almost an intellectual construct, "the flesh made word," to borrow Ed Yoder's biblical quip. Having a distinctiveness to lose makes possible a recognition of loss, and that triggers a process of retrospection and nostalgia that bodes well to keep the South alive and thriving. The South will continue to exist, if only by an act of the will. After all, as Brandt Ayers has remarked, they aren't having symposia in Phoenix to discuss the everlasting West.

The essays in this volume were originally prepared for a symposium held at Tulane University on February 6 and 7, 1981, funded in part by the Louisiana Committee for the Humanities and the National Endowment for the Humanities. The topics chosen arose from the ways the South has been comprehended by both northerners and southerners, by academic scholars and perceptive observers of various kinds. Any attempt to capture the region's identity today, to study and describe it and then ponder what the future will bring, is conditioned by earlier efforts to understand "the enigma of the South," to borrow the title of one of David Potter's essays.

Pause for a moment and consider the key images associated with the idea of the South: race, politics, a rural folk (and, correspondingly, a relative absence of large cities), an educationally and culturally benighted region, the Bible Belt, poverty along with new-fangled ideas about Sunbelt prosperity, rumors of change and a disappearing South. It was with those kinds of images in mind that the topics and speakers were chosen. Surely other appropriate topics could have been included, had time and money permitted; but those actually chosen are representative of the questions that any examination of southernness would include. The authors were given wide leeway in how they would approach their topics; they were asked to glance briefly at popular perceptions and past interpretations, then to delve into the present reality of their topics. Finally, each author was urged to speculate about the future. No attempt was made for uniformity in style, approach, definition, or interpretation. The South has always encompassed variety, efforts to squeeze it into a central theme notwithstanding; and this collective portrait of the South in an age of change mirrors that diversity. Journalists were chosen because of their ability to communicate effectively, their experience at cutting through rhetoric to reality, and their real-world experience with the topics under examination. We offer *Dixie Dateline* as an up-to-date, wide-ranging report on the South as it has been, is now, and might become.

Roy Reed opens the discussion with his analysis of the southern folk, those often-forgotten people whose influence on southern mores has been immense. Reed writes with affection and perception, and he sees the violence as well as the simple religious faith that lie entangled in the region's values. Most of the formerly rural southerners have now moved to urban areas, but their rural ways linger, and that umbilical cord to the past seems certain to nourish at least a vague sense of folk values amidst the skyscrapers and freeways of the region's boom cities.

In many ways blacks are the quintessential southerners, but their lot in the South has seldom been pleasant. If the white South saw itself as impoverished and discriminated against within the nation, black southerners were doubly cursed. Despite momentary euphoria in the movement days of the 1960s, southern blacks are now less hopeful, suggests Paul Delaney, about the future. Race relations in Dixie may have caught up with the rest of the nation, but as Delaney says, that really doesn't mean much—and may mean even less in the near future.

The intellectual and material impoverishment of southern educational institutions has long been an unwelcome cliché applied to the region. The Civil War and postbellum economic stagnation dealt southern colleges a severe blow, and late nineteenth century models of the modern university—pioneered by Johns Hopkins, Harvard, and Michigan—were slow to find adherents in the South. But as John A. Crowl shows, southern universities have begun to close the educational gap. Today a national uniformity of academic expectations—from curricula to standards for promotions—is probably more noticeable than regional variations. While no southern university has yet nudged into the company of the Harvards,

Chicagos, and Berkeleys, population and economic growth will continue to offer the states of Dixie a potential for relative improvement if their leaders have the will to demand it.

Even before H. L. Mencken derisively labeled the South the Bible Belt, it was well known that Dixie was the most religiously solid region of the nation. Three large Protestant denominations—Baptists, Methodists, and Presbyterians—had an evangelical armlock on the South, and any attempt to understand the "southern mind" must include the religious dimension. The effect on the South of this religious uniformity has been both good and bad, and now the grip of religion—and the varieties of religion—are changing as the region becomes more urban and cosmopolitan. Wilmer C. Fields portrays this important and complex subject in his essay, "On Jordan's Stormy Banks."

The ghost of H. L. Mencken sometimes seems to haunt the recent South, for his pungently expressed aphorisms for two generations have been the way that many nonsoutherners have imagined the South. On no aspect of southern deficiencies was the ascerbic Baltimorean more harsh than on her cultural attainments, by which Mencken meant high culture. Almost simultaneous with his remarks, the South began a remarkable literary movement, and we now appreciate the rich folk culture of Dixie. But simply taking Mencken on his own terms, W. L. Taitte reexamines the South's cultivation of the fine arts and finds good reasons for the region's lag in art museums and symphony orchestras sixty years ago. He points with not a little pride to the South's culture boom of today, particularly in the largest, wealthiest cities. Now the National Endowment for the Arts has announced that, based on a study of the 1980 census, the South has the largest artist population of any region.

It is only since World War II—which may be a more important turning point in southern history than even the Civil War—that the South has possessed large and wealthy cities. Rural stereotypes about the southern landscape ill prepare one to comprehend bustling Atlanta and Dallas, much less Houston, now the nation's fourth largest and fastest-growing city. Yet these shiny new cities are not obviously "southern" except in location. As Neal R. Peirce observes, there is a sameness to urban America that can be disheartening; perhaps the small southern cities—the Charlestons and

Savannahs—have been more successful in maintaining their charm as they have undergone change.

Politics of a special kind—one-party, yellow-dog Democrats, with corn-pone folk heroes and racist demagogues thrown in to add local color—has often been a defining stereotype of the South. But here too the region has been transformed by the economic, political, and racial changes following World War II. The Republican party is now alive and well in Dixie—at least among white voters—and there is at last a genuine two-party South, especially in terms of national politics.

For generations southern politicians could not realistically aspire for national office, borne down as they were by the scorn of Confederate defeat and the shame of racism. Having no national ambitions, southern politicians saw no need to address national issues, take national stands, or rise above local or provincial politics in an effort to become more than a regional candidate. Now all that has changed. Jimmy Carter showed that a southerner could become president, and the result has been a freeing of southern politicians from the limitation of reduced ambition. As Brandt Ayers shows in his essay, southern politics has been revolutionized by the black vote and the rise of a group of southern politicians who have eyes for the presidency. Several of these aspirants bear careful watching, for they are what journalists like to call "presidential timber." The southern voter needs to be approached in special ways, however, and candidates who hope to carry the region, getting both black and white votes, must be attuned to the defining characteristics of the South as a region.

Poor, backward, provincial is how the South was perceived for generations, and "hick flicks" and television series like "The Dukes of Hazzard" ensure that old stereotypes will never completely die. But the modern, urban South has moved far beyond outdated characterizations. In no part of the South has economic and population growth, combined with urbanization, effected greater changes than in the Southwest, particularly the oil-rich states of Louisiana, Oklahoma, and Texas. Fueled by oil and gas money and by substantial inmigration, a new culture—neither really southern nor exactly "national"—is emerging in what William K. Stevens calls the "oil patch." Houston has undergone the most remarkable trans-

formation. Once labeled a "whiskey and trombone town," it is now the
world center of petroleum technology and possesses one of the world's
largest, most comprehensive medical centers. Both its oil and medical expertise attract persons from around the globe, and it is also a major international port—a far cry from the isolated Houston, and the South, of sev-
enty-five years ago.

Houston is simply the most spectacular example of general economic
growth throughout the South, a development that has given rise to the
label "Sunbelt." In an incisive analysis, James R. Adams surveys both the
origins of the term and the reality of the label. He shows that indiscriminate use of the term suggests erroneously that recent economic developments are homogeneous; there are at least three different economic sub-
units within the South, and the term implies too great a causative factor to
weather. Reviewing various theories for the South's gradual closing of the
poverty gap between itself and the rest of the nation (though it is still the
nation's poorest region), Mr. Adams suggests by way of the Louisiana experience a provocative theory of his own to explain regional growth.

In the face of all this urban growth and unparalleled prosperity, native
southerners born before the end of World War II may be forgiven for
sometimes feeling that the old, comfortable, familiar South of their youth
is disappearing. Edwin M. Yoder, Jr., certainly evokes an understanding
nod of the head from readers of the requisite age when he describes the
disappearance of the Dixie of recent memory. All the old set pieces are
gone, he writes, and it is only by a conscious act of reminiscing that the
distinctly different South is kept alive by periodic resuscitation. Symposia
and collections like this, Yoder suspects, represent no less than attempts by
journalists and historians to "Dixiefy Dixie." Nevertheless, he hesitates
from actually pronouncing an epitaph for the South.

In the course of his essay, Ed Yoder pays obeisance to an influential article, "The Search for Southern Identity," published by C. Vann Woodward
in 1958. Woodward had first developed these ideas in his presidential address to the Southern Historical Association in November 1952, published
in 1953. What made the South different, Woodward argued, was its collective historical experience, an experience at variance with the nation's past

but ironically quite similar to the larger world's experience. Woodward then suggested that southerners should be able to understand non-Americans, and empathize with them, in ways beneficial both to this nation and to our global neighbors. Alas, southerners have seldom learned the lessons they should have from their past, as Hodding Carter notes in the final essay. Looking out from the South rather than at the region, Mr. Carter shows that history's lessons are less clear, and less easily accepted, than we might like to believe. Nevertheless, the South has a relevance not fully appreciated even by self-conscious southerners, and perhaps that is the reason why thoughtful people around the world maintain a fascination with things southern from Faulkner to folklore. The past does have a future.

Many persons at Tulane University made possible this symposium and the resulting essays. S. Frederick Starr, then vice-president of Tulane, suggested the initial idea for the seminar, and Sheldon Hackney, then president, gave encouragement, both intellectual and monetary. Phillip Carter of New Orleans did likewise and was especially helpful in suggesting participants. Roy Reed, along with Ray Jenkins, now of the *Baltimore Evening Sun*, also gave most helpful advice. The Tulane administration was very supportive, as was the staff of the Louisiana Committee for the Humanities, particularly Carla Geraghty and Patrice Prat. Diana Pinckley and her coworkers in the Office of University Relations at Tulane did yeoman service to publicize the event. Thanks to Dean Joseph Gordon and history department chairman Richard Greenleaf for giving me released time for planning the symposium. Pamela Tyler, my assistant on the project, was simply essential. Elaine Severio and Valleria Palo, history department sec-.retaries, cheerfully typed all the correspondence. Several colleagues at Tulane, especially Bill C. Malone and Lawrence N. Powell, contributed in a variety of ways, including commenting on the papers. Michael P. Kreyling of the Tulane English department also helped place the symposium discussions in a broader context. My new colleagues at Rice University have similarly provided an atmosphere conducive to research and publication, and Kathy Tomasic, Cathy Azzi, and Darlene U. Collins have done additional typing. Several colleagues at various institutions—Bill C. Malone, Lawrence N. Powell, Patrick Maney, D. Blake Touchstone, Samuel C. Ramer, Bennett H. Wall, Dee Pipes, Evelyn T. Nolen—and my wife Nancy have commented on and improved my introduction. Barbara Burnham of Rice University Studies has supported the final publication of the project in a number of ways. And most of all I thank the practicing journalists, the participants, who made *Dixie Dateline* a lively symposium and who contributed the essays that follow, for after all, it is their book.

☆ ☆ ☆ **1** ☆ ☆ ☆

Ab Snopes Makes Good

ROY REED

They called us trash. They had to have an explanation, and that was it. Theirs was God's own economic system and when it failed, blame had to be placed. The black slaves were easy to explain. Even the Yankees would tell you, in private, that niggers didn't amount to anything. But if the world's greatest civilization since Greece did not produce a decent living for the majority of the white folks, there had to be a reason. The fault was not in the civilization; it was in the folks. Some folks were trash.

Maybe they were right. We have never had what it takes to build plantations. We're too lazy and too anxious about the righteous wrath of God. We dislike mosquitoes and hot weather, so we have always stuck close to the top of the South in the hills and mountains. Our aspirations in the beginning ran to creek bottoms instead of river deltas. Without money, slaves, and plantations, we produced very few governors and senators, and no more sheriffs than were necessary. We spun off a few preachers and distillers, but not many others in what might be called the public service. Mostly, until the end of the nineteenth century, we farmed the hills and bottoms and stayed close to home, minding our own business.

Then the twentieth century came, and the South got serious about The American Way: industry, towns, getting ahead. The trash began to percolate and drift. Some went up and some went sideways, but all of us were in motion. Now, in the ninth decade, it is clear that this has turned out to be the century of the white trash. We have percolated and drifted from one end of the country to the other. We have captured all of the towns in the South and have established outposts as far away as Bakersfield and Detroit, and we've got our eye on New York. Wherever we have moved in with enough force, we have become the barbers, grocers, beauticians, lawyers, cooks, factory workers, postmen, nurses, junk yard operators, plumbers, car dealers, lumbermen, reporters, choir directors, television evangelists, mechanics. We are in business. We have even gone into politics and have not stopped at the rank of justice of the peace. The red-necked pecker-wood, once considered the most retiring bird in the South, has come to town and taken over.

Wherever we settle, no matter how urban the climate, we remember who we are. I know an Arkansas redneck who has lived in New York for twenty years. He is high in the editorial councils of the *New Yorker* maga-zine. He spends practically the whole of his enormous salary shuttling his sons to a place in the country to make sure they know how to fish.

Fishing. One of the many important bonds for those of us who have drifted into the towns. My Uncle Rube and I are sitting in a boat fishing a long hole of water in Irons Creek. A beaver has been slapping the water at the lower end of the hole. We have caught a few bass and bream. One of us looks up and sees Afton Ratliff walking across his pasture. He is not in a hurry, but he walks straight to the creek bank. He shouts to Rube across the water.

"Who's your man for President?"

"Wallace!"

"They just shot him!"

He goes back into the house. We go back to fishing.

Bond is not exactly the right word. Bond suggests that millions of us, as we go about our business in the cities and towns, are tied by long pieces of rope running to Aly and Buckville and Possum Kingdom, like calves staked out to graze the long grass by the highway. That is not quite accu-rate. Actually, we have brought the creeks and hollers to town with us. We are country people who now, by some historical imperative that we have not given much thought to, happen to live in town. We are slowly losing our countryness—our trashiness—and in time I guess we will lose it all.

But we have not lost it yet, and the older ones among us are as redolent of manure and catfish bait as the day we left home. We think like country people. We act like country people when we can get away with it. We are country people, for a little while longer.

How much longer depends partly on the condition of the rootstock still living in the country. Not all of us have strayed to the towns. A few have stayed at home, have been there all along, nourishing the stock that replenishes us all. Mother of vinegar—the few drops that contain the life of the entire line, and from which a new batch can be started any time.

It is the rootstock that interests me especially. I find, like most who have gone away from the country and returned, that I spend considerable time poking among the rootstock checking for soundness and rot. Or, to pursue the more complex metaphor, sniffing the vinegar and tasting the wine. People who dabble in such manufacture know that one yeast, a single wayward cousin, makes the difference between wine and vinegar. Country people have no use for wine.

Call him Tom. He is that similar to a cat. Elastic, crazy, night-stirring, fired by vinegar, impelled toward risk. His people have lived on the western slope of the Ozarks for generations. The community wisdom is that Tom is the end of the line. As a species, they say, he is as endangered as the cougar that George Penny, aged ten, reported during last year's deer hunt, or the black bear that Ancel Waterson saw walking a dirt road on Webber Mountain last winter.

Tom makes the theory reasonable. He almost cut his leg off with a chain saw in a fit of carelessness. He once went to the hospital for a serious, undiagnosed illness, and when the doctors wired him with tubes and electrodes, he waited until he was alone, unplugged himself, and went home. A year ago, at the age of twenty-one, he mortgaged the remainder of his life to buy a farm, then lost interest in it in six months. He bought an almost-wrecked car one day, and with a case of beer and a band of friends, took it to a brushy, stump-warted clearing in the woods and drove it to death in one voluptuous night.

He got married—not from choice but because he had knocked the girl up. His nights became as listless as his days. He stirred himself only once more. He announced that he had heard of a fantastic job in western Oklahoma, five hundred miles away, and he got into his pickup and left. The betting was that the community and his wife had seen the last of him. He came back two days later. We are waiting now to record his extinction. Will it come slowly, spinning out the useless time, or quickly, like a whippoorwill dashing itself against a window? It is easy to portray Tom as a metaphor: the last of the white trash, threatened by forces he does not understand, unable to deal with the new reality, turning inward finally to destroy himself. It is easy, and I am half persuaded that it is true.

I have seen Ozark people shouldered aside and shoved into the more remote land by retired Yankees. I have seen Louisiana Cajuns infiltrated and changed by Texas oilmen, and gullah-talking Carolinians altered and pushed out of the marshes by retired generals. I have seen all of the backcountry southerners from Florida crackers to Tennessee hillbillies cheapened, deceived, and changed forever by television, interstate highways, throwaway plastics, and double-knit preachers from California. All of us have seen the real estate speculators and the corporate owners of woods and farms push the price of land so high that no one, no matter how skillful—certainly not the likes of Tom—will ever again be able to buy a farm and pay for it from its own produce. We have seen the search for a radical alternative, the desperate youngsters from the city going south to the hills to establish a new way, self-sufficiency from the land. Most leave during the first winter. Those who stay end up supporting themselves with menial jobs in the towns and become self-sufficient only in home-grown marijuana.

Tom's people are threatened all across the South. They are the red men who no longer remember how to hunt.

I recently sat beside a hospital bed with five aging women waiting for one of them to go into surgery.

One of them said, "Do y'all remember that girl that married the Richardson boy?"

"Wasn't that Emmie Lou Smith?"

"No, Emmie Lee Smith married Jim McClellan. I'm talking about that girl with the crooked leg. She married that Richardson boy from the Holler."

"No, she didn't. I know who you're talking about. She married Odell Blocker, and they had that boy that had to go to the penitentiary."

They moved on without me, snipping and picking to untangle the memory of who was sister to whom, who the father, who the husband. And weren't they kin to us somehow on the Melton side? They talked with a curious insistence, as if the tangle needed to be dealt with before the sick woman, who was sister to two of them and double first cousin to the other two, went into the operating room.

I had heard the same conversation all my life, with only the names shifted from one gathering to the next. Suddenly I sat marvelling at the strength of the past. In the hills, the past is personal. The conversation of my Grandfather Meredith, whose memory ran to the 1880s, was always about family and people—our people. He might recall a spectacular crop, or the killing of a neighbor, but he almost never spoke of public events beyond our community. He did occasionally talk of the First World War, but only as it affected some young man of the community. One fellow, for example, had shot a toe off to avoid the draft. Another had fought in France; a fine fellow, one of the best shots with a rifle you ever saw.

I never heard him mention the Civil War unless someone asked a question about it. No one in our family talked of the Civil War. When we did mention it, we never called it the War Between the States. Our people had fought in it, and with considerable interest, I'm sure. How could they fail to be interested when the bloodiest event of their time rolled right over them? One great-uncle was wounded at Vicksburg. But it was not our war and our people knew it. I now live within ten miles of a famous battlefield, a place in the Ozarks where the armies of the North and the South happened to come together. The people here speak of the place as they might of a spot on the highway where two carloads of strangers collided. A few families of the nearby towns work to keep the memory alive, and the county historical association invests a lot of time and sentiment in it. But the past of the country people is invested elsewhere. Among hillbillies, the past is a family affair.

Our own family, like many others, is scattered now. It ranges from Fresno to Madrid, with a large representation at Hot Springs, the town nearest its Arkansas root. (The main root runs across the southern uplands to the Appalachians, and thence to Ulster, Scotland, and England. Or so we think. We are not much given to genealogy.)

Only a handful are left in the back reaches of the Ouachita Mountains where the root first put down in Arkansas. On the side of my mother's people, the Merediths and Meltons, the country survivors are huddled around a community called Mount Tabor in northern Garland County. My father's people settled a few miles away in southern Yell County, at a place called Aly. The Reeds were a large, scrappy, yellow-headed family, and they scrambled out of Yell County by the dozens during the Great Depression. They went to Texas, Colorado, California, anywhere that promised work and the seductive fripperies of civilization. The men had seen Henry Ford's astonishing creation, and the women had access to the Sears & Roebuck catalog.

Of all the dozens who left, only one of the Reeds came back to Yell County to retire, many years later. He found just one living relic of the family when he got back. Just one man had stayed behind, out of all the Reeds who sprang there, and he did not call himself Reed.

But first, Mount Tabor. Small-time farming community, much like hundreds of other hill hamlets from Arkansas to Virginia. The only public buildings are a tiny store at the top of the hill and a church and graveyard down by the creek. The church is Baptist. (Notice how like Papist the word sounds.) Several of its preachers have been kin to me. Half the occupants of the graveyard are, too, and the same can be said of the graveyard at Aly four or five mountains away.

The living population of Mount Tabor consists of a few dozen farm families, including a number of Meltons and Merediths. Everybody at Mount Tabor is white and has been since the Indians retired 150 years ago. A few slaves were kept on the larger farms in the Ouachita River bottoms ten or fifteen miles away, and a few of their descendants lived there when I was a child. Some member of our family would see one from time to time, maybe once a year, and the event would be discussed for days. The government dammed the Ouachita about forty years ago and flooded everybody out, black and white. Our family saw a lot of black people after that, on the streets of Hot Springs among other cities. It was at Hot Springs that I first saw a black person. I was four years old. We were visiting Aunt Sue Meredith. One of the women took me to a front window and pointed to a man walking past. He wore shabby clothes. His face was strange in a way that did not register until later. The women told me that he was the Sack Man. I remember the chill. The Sack Man worked for the Devil, known to me as the Booger Man, and for small children he had one role. "The Sack Man will get you if you don't behave."

Mount Tabor bustled once, not with business but with small farms. The hollows and creek bottoms were settled thickly with families; each one tilled twenty or thirty acres to grow corn, oats, and kitchen vegetables. A family usually grew a little cotton for cash. Not much cotton was left in the hills by 1940, nor many people. The depression thinned Mount Tabor as a farmer thins corn. My Grandfather Meredith hung on until World War II, then gave up and moved to Hot Springs to work as a carpenter. All of his five children had left before him.

Those who stayed in the country, including several of my cousins at Mount Tabor, took up the slack in an interesting way. At first, the newly urbanized cousins looked down at those they had left behind. The feeling was that if they had amounted to anything, if they had had any get-up-and-go, they would have moved to town and made money. Then, after a few years, the town cousins began to notice that the country cousins were doing quite well. They had annexed the land left by the emigrants, and some had become the owners of rather large acreages. The male cousins who had moved to town always went home several times a year to hunt. Before long, the returning hunters began to yearn for what they had left behind. Now and again one would inquire discreetly about land for sale back home. Would George Tom be interested in selling a few acres of the old family land back to one of the town cousins? The cousin thought it might be nice to have a hunting cabin on the old place. Or maybe he would run a few head of cattle and get a neighbor to look after them. Late at night, around the hunters' fire, he would ask whether they knew what he would really like to do, and they would say no, and he would say, "What I'd really like to do someday is get me a place and move back up here." The country cousins would say what a fine thing that would be, and he would talk himself into a state of excitement at the prospect.

But he never made it back. He could not whip his own inertia and his wife's reluctance. He owned a late-model car, and he noticed that his cousin, for all his envied land, rattled around in a worn-out pickup. The town wife had an automatic washing machine; the country wife did the washing by hand, on a rub board. So he went on working ten hours a day clerking in the hardware store, or selling $500 burial insurance policies, or struggling to scrape up enough money to buy his own grocery store. And back home at Mount Tabor his cousin added two or three head of cattle to his herd each year to take the place of the abandoned cotton and sold a little pine timber to Dierks Lumber Company, and during a good year he would pipe water into the house or build on a new room or buy another fifteen acres from a neighbor.

Thus was the mother of vinegar preserved. They are still there, minor squires overseeing a new rural community: city people retired on five acres; young town couples in house trailers commuting twenty miles to work; fishing camp and motel operators; and, strewn ever thinner, a hand-ful of the offspring of the original stock, just enough to keep the vinegar alive.

The country trash are not all prospering. It is easy to find pockets of economic evil—the old miners with no coal left and too little land, and scattered others who prefer to stretch the welfare check in the country rather than in some mean city street. Drive any highway through the hills and you will see half a dozen littered hovels in a fifteen-mile ride. These are the Toms of this generation, the hillbilly minority who still fit the label and who are steadily dying out, year by year, making space for the more adapt-able, native and outlander.

Most of the heirs of the people they called white trash are now doing well where they have clung to the land. Better than the heirs of the slaves. The black southerners who stayed in the country are now two distinct classes: on the one hand those who work for the white landowners in the Deep South, tractor drivers, now paid fairly well (men like the last share-cropper on Jimmy Carter's family plantation, who earns as much as a college teacher and owns several rent houses in Plains), and on the other hand the castoffs who have no work and no income except welfare and who live in semiwildness in stinking shanties at the edges of the old farms and villages.

The surviving country white people—not the gentility of the Deep South but the ordinary people of the foothills and the mountains—are now generally comfortable. They live in new or fixed-up houses, many of them ranch-style brick. They drive late model cars and pickups. The children still at home have their own vehicles. Campers and boats are parked in the yards. Their kitchens are modern, and their televisions are in color. They spend a lot of money on expensive guns and fishing tackle. They travel a little, usually to popular fishing and hunting spots.

They are public spirited, in a narrow fashion. They support the church. One of my Meredith cousins sits on the school board of the new Jessieville consolidated district, even though he and his wife have no children. They are meticulous in maintaining the old graveyards. They speak out on public issues in a selective way, shyly, uncomfortable at having their opinions and thoughts revealed. When the United States Forest Service and one of the big timber companies began clear-cutting the woods around Mount Tabor, the Merediths swallowed their shyness and spoke their anger to newspaper reporters. The clear-cutting went on, as they knew it would, and they did not mention it again except among the family.

They do not think of it as public service, but they keep alive for a while longer some of the fading country skills. An occasional fiddler and banjo player still hold out against television. They make gardens and cut firewood. Here and there is an old-timer who remembers how to butcher a hog. Many cattlemen are as skilled as veterinarians in emergencies in the herd.

The survival of the old skills is one of the main reasons for the specialness that sets apart and gives value to the remaining country people. In my own adopted community there lives a man, now seventy, who spends a fair percentage of his time advising the young and newcomers on how to live in the country—how to brace a fence post, how to castrate a calf, how to find the best place to drill a well.

At least one other surviving quality sets the native country people apart and makes them special. I used to think of it often when I worked in Washington and Atlanta and in the cities and villages of Britain and Ireland. It is a quality of community that goes deeper than a name. Hogeye, Arkansas, is not merely a place name or a dateline. It is a community in a way that is difficult to imagine among city people. The secret of the hill-country community—and most other rural communities that I have known—is a profound interdependence that has nothing to do with do-goodery or sentimentalism, or even religion. Country people look after one another. They have always done so. The trash take care of their own, not out of goodness but out of necessity. There is no one else to do it. If I have to have help lifting a rock out of my pasture or starting a contrary tractor engine, I do not call for a Kelly Girl; I call for Seth Timmons or Norman Findahl. If Seth needs help overhauling a motor, he does not call the Ford dealer; he calls Jim Winn. That is the simple dictate of economics when you live long, expensive miles from the nearest town.

The benefits go beyond economics. People specially value those whom they depend upon and who depend upon them in return. For that and other reasons, the active shareholders in a community, the daily participants in its ups and downs, tragedies and titillations, are drawn close to history. They feel not only the undead past every day but also the present as it treads to keep abreast of history's current. Hogeye does not profess to be concerned with the great sweeps of the world's story. History here is more personal. I replace a weathered old plank on my barn and the plank ties me to the day when Seth Timmons nailed it to what was then his barn. Seth pulls an onion from his garden and feels a tug from the past. This year's crop is the latest in a hardy line of multipliers that his Grandmother Timmons brought in a tow sack from Tennessee in the 1800s.

City people looking for five acres and retirement paradise are beginning to distort the history and dilute the specialness of places like Hogeye and Mount Tabor. But the specialness will be with us awhile longer, as long as the rootstock and the multiplier onions survive.

The price of specialness is high. Hill politics, for example, are an extension of the rural acquisitive instinct. Not a hill farmer ever lived who did not covet his neighbor's land. Those who thrive in the country are those who know how to get and keep. They do not believe in giving their gain away in welfare money, or even in elemental taxation. They see no need for frills like food stamps. Schools and even roads are supported grudgingly.

Hill people look with suspicion on genuine higher education, anything that emphasizes the arts and sciences at the expense of football. Many of the young go away to college now, and when they occasionally acquire the rudiments of an education they find that an unbridgeable gap has opened between them and the people back home. They usually move on, talking vaguely of greener pastures.

Among those they leave behind, the circle of perspective expands far, far slower than it might in an urban place. The mind that is suspicious of education is also suspicious of distant places, people, and ideas. In a way, an Ozarks mountaineer is as limited in his outlook as any Manhattan cab driver.

Hill people are contentious, in spite of their abiding sense of community. They love a feud. A new family moved into our community recently, and the wife let it be known that she preferred reading to visiting and did not appreciate neighbors dropping in unannounced. We are leaving her alone with satisfaction. Every community needs someone to point a hostile finger at. At Mount Tabor, one of my cousins fell out with her brothers over an inheritance or a piece of property or something of the sort, and they have been feuding contentedly for fifteen years.

We are strict constructionists in the interpretation of God's will. In one community only the Baptists are considered safe from Hell, and in another only the Presbyterians or the Pentecostals. The only major doctrine that all rural Protestants agree on is that the Roman Catholic Church is obnoxious to the Lord. One of my earliest memories is of sermons denouncing the

Catholics. I remember the fear and revulsion I felt the first time I walked past St. John's Catholic Church in Hot Springs. It was the same fear and revulsion that I had felt for the Sack Man in front of Aunt Sue's house. Years later, in the late 1970s, I encountered the same feelings among the fundamentalist Protestants of Northern Ireland, and suddenly I knew where we had learned to hate.

The hatred finally withered in one small branch of my family. My Grandmother Meredith died a slow death of cancer, and she spent her last three months in St. Joseph's Hospital at Hot Springs. The hospital is run by nuns. One elderly nun looked after my grandmother, visiting her several times every day, attending her suffering and her most unpleasant—you might say repulsive—disrupted functions. The two old women came to love each other. One day near the end, the old nurse said, "You are such a good patient." My grandmother replied, "No, Sister"—the very word would once have gagged her—"you are the one who's good."

One more thing has to be said about our specialness. We have a streak of plain damned meanness, and it is as much a part of our history as multiplier onions. Our ancestors posted signs at the railroad stops saying, "Nigger Don't Let The Sun Set On You Here." They enforced the policy with clubs and guns, because we have always loved violence. A hillbilly hunter will kill a dozen squirrels from a den tree—old, young, suckling mothers and all. He does not need that many for food. He simply likes to shoot living creatures.

I once talked to a teen-aged boy in Stone County, Arkansas, who had been shot by his grandfather. He and several other boys had gone to the old man's yard to play a Halloween prank. The man opened the door and blazed away with buckshot. He knew that one of the boys was his own grandson.

The hills exact a kind of justice. I will tell you about a great uncle of mine who was moderately wicked and died poor, or so he thought. Uncle Josh (the name is fiction, out of deference to certain kin who might still care) was one of a huge clan of Reeds in the rocky hills of Yell County. Like many modern farmers, Uncle Josh had an independent source of income. My own is a typewriter. His was a whisky still. He liked women as well as he liked whisky, and in illicit cohabitation with a neighbor girl he produced an additional heir. The child had his mother's name, but everybody knew he was Joshua Reed's boy. He was treated as you would expect a bastard child to be treated in Yell County, Arkansas, in the first decades of the twentieth century—like trash. That put him in the same class with the rest of the Reeds in the eyes of the delta planters.

All of the other Reeds pulled out of Yell County during the 1930s and 1940s. They laid it to the depression, but the reason was older than that. They left to go to Gomorrah. They had heard of the finery there, linoleum rugs and Ford cars and jobs that paid fifteen dollars a week. In Gomorrah, they did not have to sweat in the fields until sundown. Someone else milked the cows, milled the meal, and butchered the pork. Life in the hills had been especially hard on the women. They fought back bitterly when the men, once lured to town, cast reappraising eyes toward home and talked of moving back where they belonged. As for the men, they became a lost generation once they left the hills. They died too young, beaten to death by sidewalks and store counters, by baffled anger, by strange language and clever city ways. Of the five women who sat with me recently in St. Joseph's Hospital, four had outlived the men who came with them from the hills. They are buried, all four men, in a Hot Springs cemetery called Memorial Gardens. It is tended and mowed by hired strangers.

Uncle Josh's unnamed boy never managed to escape from Yell County. While the others left, he stayed and fretted with his shame and with the sorry, worn-out land. He bought a few acres, somehow. People were selling eagerly to the timber companies and the Forest Service. Thousands of acres were taken permanently out of circulation in Yell County during the depression. Uncle Josh's boy could not compete with the big-time buyers and the government, but he held on to what he had and added more from time to time. About twenty years ago he got my grandfather's forty acres, where my father and ten brothers and sisters were born. He turned the abandoned log house into a hay barn. He now owns every scrap of Reed land in Aly, Arkansas, and more besides. His herd of cattle is one of the largest in that part of the state. As a gesture of something, he gave my grandfather's old log house to one of my uncles to be moved, rebuilt, and preserved as a kind of memento on a suburban lot at Little Rock. Nothing he has done has made him respectable, of course. But he is accepted as a man of substance, and I suppose that is more than he hoped for.

He has one other consolation. The mother of vinegar resides in him, and he knows it. He also knows where he will be buried. They will put him under a cedar tree in the Aly Graveyard, a few steps from his daddy.

☆ ☆ ☆ **2** ☆ ☆ ☆

A New South for Blacks?

PAUL DELANEY

To appreciate the differences in feelings about the South by white southerners and black southerners, one need only play "Dixie" or wave a Confederate flag. Whites, many of them, respond with rebel yells; blacks, almost unanimously, flinch, finding the old symbols detestable. At the moment the South is enjoying an unprecedented boom, thanks to the bless-
ings that flow to the Sunbelt. That prosperity has led blacks to tone down
their deep, negative feelings, and the tide of black migration has turned
back toward the South. Dixie, however, still evokes mixed emotions for
black Americans. The "New South" has not erased the fact that the Old
South was unkind to the blacks to whom it gave birth but nurtured inade-
quately. The result has been a continuing love-hate relationship. On the
one hand, the South is a land of new opportunity for blacks. But it also
carries the legacy of bloody racial confrontations, lynchings, and deaths
that are etched in the memory of the region's black citizens. Martin Luther
King, Birmingham, Selma, Medgar Evers, Goodman, Chaney, Schwerner,
Emmett Till, the Scottsboro Boys. . . . The list goes on.

The region of opportunity is a place of contradiction. Blacks returning
"home" find remnants of segregation; lingering racism remains part of the
landscape. Yet many are frustrated with the way things have turned out in
the northern states, which received them with open arms when they were
denied by their native land and are now fueling the great return. Some of
the same highways that took blacks north a generation or so ago are now

speeding them back home. Earlier in this century blacks fled the often painful reality of the South, seeking the promise of equality, justice, and jobs in a North that was an image of deliverance to them.

The South of today is as much image now as the North once was, an image that has been bought by black and white southerners alike. It is a source of pride for them all. For blacks who arrived in Chicago or Detroit a generation ago and worked to lose the drawl, learn "proper" English, and do all they could to hide their southern background, southern pride is a new phenomenon. White southerners are cultivating their southernness defiantly, especially in the North, but black southerners are also subtly evincing a sense of belonging to the region. Both races exhibit pride in celebrating the South through "home town" clubs in major cities, including New York and Chicago. It is acceptable, even fashionable, to eat southern cooking (white) and soul food (black), or at least to claim that one does if one is from the South. The North has been invaded by southern ways, southern culture, from Broadway and Times Square to residential neighborhoods across the region. Broadway has always been fascinated by things southern. But grits on menus in Times Square? (They could always be found in Harlem restaurants.) White Mississippians now hold an annual Mississippi Day in Central Park.

Despite racially-oriented conflicts, black and white southerners share many similarities attributable to their regional background. They are deeply religious, even though their churches mean different things to the two races (black churches are more activist, white churches more fundamentalist). They share conservative views on many moral issues, though blacks are more tolerant of abortion and out-of-wedlock births, for example. They have strong attachments to family, friends, and community. These are the classic ingredients for making a southerner.

Nevertheless, the differences stand out and distinguish white southerners from black southerners. In listening to their diction, it is easier to tell whether a white person is from Alabama, Georgia, North Carolina, Tennessee, or Kentucky than a black person from those same states, although on occasion even a trained ear cannot distinguish a white from a black southerner simply by accent. But views on race and racial history are still the strongest distinguishing characteristics between the two. The historical marker for that difference and for modern race relations, the "New South," and the future of relations remains the civil rights movement of the 1960s.

We who twenty years ago were reporters, observers, or supporters of the movement were fully aware of the significance of the period. We were all, in one way or another, caught up in the emotionalism of the day. But preoccupied with a revolution in progress, we had little time—or did not take the time—to think too deeply about where it was headed; we dreamed more of where we wished it to go.

Compared to the rest of the South, Atlanta, where I lived, was a mecca. It was a racial heaven, as well as a haven, compared to Birmingham, Selma, Montgomery, and the whole of Mississippi, among other places. The response to demonstrations by Atlanta municipal officials and police was markedly different from that in most other cities. There was no "Bull" Connor or Jim Clark or Laurie Pritchett in the Georgia capital. It was spared the extreme tension, violence, and racist resistance that surrounded the movement. The city's enlightened and sophisticated black middle class had much to do with that attitude. That elite cadre complemented its liberal white counterpart. The alliance flourished not out of a sense of morality, but out of concern for maintaining the city's image and favorable business climate, which meant preventing avowed segregationists, such as Lester Maddox, from coming to power and upsetting the delicate balance. Atlanta was the staging ground, as well as the center of rest and recuperation, for legions of black and white warriors sent to battle the philistines of segregation.

It was a period of joining hands and swaying to the slow, rhythmic beat of the movement's theme song: "We shall overcome. . . . We shall overcome someday. . . . Black and white together. . . ." It was a ritual that excited the heart, that seldom failed to draw a tear. It was a period of intense emotions. It was a time of joy, but also of sadness; it was a time of optimism, and of setbacks.

True, the big war over segregation was won nonviolently. There was exultation in 1963 when Martin Luther King, Jr., revealed his dream, and in 1964 when Congress enacted and President Lyndon B. Johnson signed into law the most sweeping civil rights legislation up to that time. But after the rejoicing was over, reality set in. The victors turned and looked at each other and were amazed to find that after all their effort, they had only scratched the surface merely to expose the most vulnerable and expendable layer of the skin of racism. And then they made the worst—and perhaps the most unforgivable—mistake of all: in an immature reaction, they blamed each other, cursed one another, and walked away from each other. And to this day, they have not been able to come together again.

As we proceed, somewhat in disarray, into the decade of the 1980s, the races are still far apart, perhaps more so than at any time since the movement. The beliefs of George Wallace, so far, have withstood the test of history better than those of Dr. King. While Governor Wallace's cry, "Segregation today, segregation tomorrow, segregation forever," demonstrated that he was not a prophet, he nevertheless struck a chord and found a chorus of followers and imitators, many of them in political offices from the courthouse to Congress to the White House. Some of his principles and policies have become the nation's principles and policies, while Dr. King's dream that freedom ring from every hilltop and every mountain remains elusive to the masses of black people in the South, as well as in the rest of the country.

Unquestionably, the days since Dr. King was killed and Governor Wallace was confined to a wheelchair have seen some profound changes in the South; the most obvious is desegregated public facilities. In addition, as a result of the Voting Rights Act, the number of black elected officials has risen dramatically and has radically changed southern politics. The number of blacks in college and with college degrees continues to increase steadily. Blacks are now cashiers at those desegregated lunch counters and in other stores and shops; school integration in the South seems more extensive than in the North, although there are still signs of widespread resegregation. Moreover, in what appears to be a good example of the fruits of the trickle-down theory, a few blacks are in some sectors of the private workplace in white collar and professional jobs, such as the media, and attend social, cultural, and political gatherings where they were not allowed a decade or so ago.

The South has made tremendous strides in race relations since I was a boy in Montgomery and a professional journalist in Atlanta. The fact that random lynchings of blacks have practically ceased qualifies as progress. Additionally, the South certainly has reached parity with the North and the rest of the country in race relations and treatment of its black citizens. In politics, Mississippi and Louisiana lead the nation in the number of blacks holding elected public office, according to the Joint Center for Political Studies in Ann Arbor. In the 1980 elections, those two states paced the country in the increase in blacks holding elected positions, followed by a third state from the region: Texas. However, the gains were the result of numerical strength rather than racial goodwill or improved relations between blacks and whites. If anything, the figures should be significantly higher, not only in Louisiana and Mississippi but throughout the Old Confederacy.

Indiscriminate violence by whites against blacks is no longer common in the South, although old fears and suspicions linger. Chet Fuller, a black Atlanta journalist who in 1978 traveled through the South disguised as an unskilled worker to experience firsthand the changed racial climate, told the story of his second-hand car breaking down one night on a lonely stretch of Interstate Highway 85 in rural North Carolina. Walking to a gas station for help and seeing inside a group of obvious "rednecks," Fuller was struck with terror. Images of killed "niggers," blacks beaten senseless, castrated, never heard from again, raced through his mind. As one of the whites towed his car to another station, Fuller sat planning how he would fight back when the evil racist tried to kill him. But the tow-truck driver delivered him to the other station where another lower-income white mechanic fixed his car cheaply and quickly and sent him on his way. Fuller's fears proved unfounded, and he was almost ashamed of having thought the worst of the economically and educationally deprived whites who had helped him. "But the truth is," he wrote, "that even though I felt foolish for being afraid, and felt a deep sickness in the pit of my stomach because of the fear that had been inside me, I could have acted in no other way. Even in 1978—after the civil-rights movement, the black movement, voting rights; after all the things that were supposed to help remove the veil of ignorance and darkness from the South—I still did not feel safe traveling alone in a car in my native region. And no other black person I knew felt any safer."[1]

When I said that the South had reached parity with the rest of the nation in race relations, it was as much a condemnation as a compliment. Being equal to the North in the treatment of blacks hardly qualifies as an accomplishment nowadays. The North's reputation and positive racial climate were inflated in the first place, camouflaging a racism deep in its fervor.

At a seminar held at the University of Mississippi a few years ago, Lerone Bennett, Jr., the black historian, answered the question asked in the theme of the meeting, "Have We Overcome?" "No," he said, "a thousand times no." "As a matter of fact," he continued, "we haven't even defined what we must do in order to overcome."[2] Bennett also charged that the race question was a white problem, not a black one, "and we shall not overcome until we confront that problem."[3]

The country has to face honestly and ultimately has to deal with the fact that the great majority of whites do not particularly care for blacks, and more and more the feeling is mutual among blacks. That dislike, in many areas, borders on pure hatred. Unless and until Americans come to grips with and overcome that phenomenon, the country will always have a race problem. The black situation is portrayed as grave and the object of conspiracy by Samuel F. Yette in his book, *The Choice: The Issue of Black Survival in America*. He maintains that blacks are obsolete in today's white America. I don't think there is a general scheme for black genocide, as Yette thinks, although there are recurring incidents that cause more than a few blacks to wonder.

Black literature has addressed the historical disdain that whites have held for blacks. Perhaps the most well known was Ralph Ellison's description of the black as "Invisible Man":

1. Chet Fuller, *I Hear Them Calling My Name: A Journey Through the New South* (Boston: Houghton Mifflin, 1981), p. 24.

2. Lerone Bennett, Jr., "Have We Overcome?" in *Have We Overcome?: Race Relations Since Brown*, ed. Michael V. Namorato (Jackson: University Press of Mississippi, 1979), p. 191.

3. Ibid., p. 200.

I am an invisible man. No, I am not a spook like those who haunted Edgar Allen Poe; nor am I one of your Hollywood-movie ectoplasms. I am a man of substance, of flesh and bone, fiber and liquids—and I might even be said to possess a mind. I am invisible, simply because people refuse to see me. Like the bodiless heads you see sometimes in circus sideshows, it is as though I have been surrounded by mirrors of hard, distorting glass. When they approach me they only see my surroundings, themselves, or figments of their imagination—indeed, everything and anything except me.[4]

That was written in 1947, and blacks are largely still invisible to the average white American, except in a negative context.

In 1955 James Baldwin echoed the theme in *Notes of a Native Son:*

One may say that the Negro in America does not really exist except in the darkness of our minds.

This is why his history and his progress, his relationship to all other Americans, has been kept in the social arena. He is a social and not personal or human problem; to think of him is to think of statistics, slums, rapes, injustices, remote violence; it is to be confronted with an endless cataloguing of losses, gains, skirmishes; it is to feel virtuous, outraged, helpless, as though his continuing status among us were somehow analogous to disease—cancer, perhaps, or tuberculosis—which must be checked even though it cannot be cured. In this arena the black man acquires quite another aspect from that which he has in life. We do not know what to do with him in life; if he breaks our sociological and sentimental image of him we are panic-stricken and we feel ourselves betrayed. When he violates this image, therefore, he stands in his greatest danger (sensing which, we easily suspect that he is playing a part for our benefit); and, what is not always so apparent but is equally true, we are then in some danger ourselves—hence our blind and immediate retaliation.[5]

4. Ralph Ellison, *Invisible Man* (New York: Random House, 1952 edition), p. 1.

5. James Baldwin, *Notes of a Native Son* (New York: Dial Press, 1963 edition), pp. 23–24.

My point in citing a few gems from black literary history is to show that those strong views of the past are just as prominent today. Although there are no lynchings as in the days of Ellison and Baldwin, and overt relations between the races have moderated in the South, there is still anger and hostility among blacks over their treatment by whites. While blacks are comforted by the changes that have taken place, there is wide belief that the root of the problem is the refusal of white Americans to acknowledge that we live in a racist society, and then do something about it.

School integration doesn't work because whites don't want it to, and they therefore torpedo busing plans and court orders to effect desegregation. Yet blacks are told it is not racism. Blacks are denied access to adequate housing, but whites deny that racism is the reason. Blacks are the victims of job discrimination, but whites reject methods, such as affirmative action and quotas, that would provide relief.

And I'm afraid that the South, despite all its resources and its place in the Sunbelt at the moment, will continue to perpetuate much of the same bitter experience that drove so many of its black sons and daughters north in search of freedom and a decent life. My own family was part of that exodus, abandoning Alabama for Ohio. I salute the progress that the South has made, but the curse of racism remains much a part of daily life. In many cases, it is more subtle, indirect, and sophisticated than the heavy-handed Jim Crow of the past. But it is just as demoralizing and deadly.

Bill Wilkenson is pilot of his own plane and wears three-piece suits with button-down-collar shirts—not exactly what one would expect of a Ku Klux Klan leader. David Duke, who once headed a Louisiana Klan group, was an articulate spokesman for the Kluxers. A history graduate of Louisiana State University, he was once described in an article as the Klan's answer to Robert Redford. Wilkenson and Duke don't fit the image of the traditional redneck Klansman, and sometimes they don't act like it. However, they are not the real concern of blacks. They are mere symbols of the neo-racism that is spreading even among those who were sympathetic to the plight of blacks sometime in the past.

Anxiety in the black community now focuses even on Washington, where the politics of Ronald Reagan's administration are considered detrimental to the interests and well-being of black America. Emma Rothschild of the Massachusetts Institute of Technology summed up the prospects in an article in the *New York Review of Books* when she wrote:

> Mr. Reagan has an imposing vision of the country that he has to lead. He sees an inherent America—an America which is white, and male, and industrial—and a project, of economic growth, by which this reality can be born again. He sees a "spirit" which is "still there, ready to blaze into life" if we stimulate our economy, increase productivity, and put America back to work. But his America no longer exists. The pursuit of his vision may lead to an economic crisis and a level of unemployment in comparison with which the events of 1975 and 1980 will appear as the merest disturbances of a compassionate state. . . . We need not doubt the new government's resolution to kick the poor by eliminating social programs.[6]

At this point, though the judgment might change in the future, the actions of the Reagan administration seem to be bearing out the worst fears of Emma Rothschild and others, myself included. Reaganomics has meant, whether intentionally or not, retrogression in the gains in race relations, more stress on blacks and whites alike, and more tension between them. The president's budget proposals and his promulgation of a "new federalism" have put tremendous strains on the poor and minorities. He has, despite promises otherwise, provided tax benefits to the middle- and upper-income earners and attempted to build up defense at the expense of the poor. Some of his nominations and appointments have been outright insults to minorities and the cause of civil rights, at least from the perspective of blacks. His support of tax exemptions for segregated schools and some of his other anti–civil rights actions were borderline racism that embarrassed even some of his white Republican constituents. That his administration has abandoned enforcement of many civil rights laws already on the books could be construed as support of racist elements in society. Even if the administration proves to be moderately successful in its economic

6. Emma Rothschild, "Reagan and the Real America," *New York Review of Books* 28 (February 5, 1981):12.

policy, racial antagonism will remain because of institutional racism, the subtlety of neo-racism, and the lack of sophistication, capability, or desire of the Reagan administration to deal with the problem. This administration is not a leader in trying to change the minds and actions of white America. On the contrary, many whites voted for Ronald Reagan in hopes that he would put a check on blacks.

This is a harsh judgment of the Reagan administration, but it is one shared by many minorities. Whether or not this view is moderated by later events, it is at present helping to shape black attitudes toward the future in general, toward the South, and toward the nation. Before there can be genuine progress, white attitudes about race and integration will have to change. The policies of the Reagan administration suggest to many blacks that white racism still lies just beneath a thin veneer of racial civility. Most whites seem able to swallow integration in small doses: one black in the neighborhood, one on the job, one black child in a classroom. The presence of two or more blacks, and surely in numbers that put whites in the minority, is seen as a threat. If the South can counter that psychology, it will have made an everlasting contribution to racial understanding. Perhaps the South can solve the problem, for its heritage of person-to-person relationships, its aversion to abstractions, and its commitment to good manners suggest that people should be respected as individuals.

Changes will also have to be made in institutions, but I don't see much evidence that they will occur voluntarily—thus the need for affirmative action and governmental nudging. Dwight D. Eisenhower might have been correct (I don't agree, though) in saying that you can't legislate morality. But it is the role of government to assure access to jobs, decent housing, a better life for all its citizens; morality will take care of itself. Witness the acceptance of blacks at lunch counters or on sports teams in the South, even in George Wallace's Alabama, where the University of Alabama has fielded an all-black starting lineup in basketball.

The primary failure of the First Reconstruction was in not providing blacks with economic as well as political power. The mistakes have been repeated ever since, and it appears that we are doomed to experience them again.

The only dependable ally that blacks have had in recent decades has been the federal government. Private sector businesses and institutions have failed miserably. White workers have historically held almost exclusively the jobs that were high paying, skilled, secure, involved authority, and led to promotion. That pattern has changed only slightly, and I'm not encouraged that the "New South" will alter it significantly. Therefore, we can expect more violent reaction of the type seen in the riots in Miami and the Klan killings in Greensboro. No black leader has emerged to replace Martin Luther King, Jr., and the unity of the black movement has been fractured, perhaps permanently. Some educated, affluent blacks who have succeeded professionally now disdain their unfortunate brothers and sisters, and class division has arisen in the black community. There are even arguments that some black government bureaucrats prosper by virtue of maintaining a black welfare class. Whites should not point accusing fingers at upwardly mobile blacks who appear to have forgotten their roots, for the successful blacks are in many ways simply following the white path to success.

I am not the optimist I was twenty years ago as a young reporter in Atlanta. I see the future of race relations in the South, and the nation, as bleak. I don't believe that the status of the masses, especially the poor, will improve appreciably in the near future. I think the system, as always, is elastic enough to allow a minimum number of us in, enough to keep most of us unrealistically hopeful. Some gains were made in the 1960s and 1970s, but the politics and economics of the 1980s appear destined to erase those gains. The nation may be more divided by both race and class in the near future than it has in the past. And that bodes ill for the entire social fabric.

Facing the Yankees Across the Education Gap

JOHN A. CROWL

Southern education—the very words conjure up a host of conflicting images:

Run-down one-room schoolhouses overflowing with poor sharecroppers' children.

Antebellum laws forbidding formal education for blacks.

White-columned finishing schools for genteel young southern ladies.

Shabby schools for "nigras," separate and obviously not equal to "white" schools.

Impoverished but literate teachers struggling against long odds to impart some wisdom to their charges.

George Wallace standing in the schoolhouse door.

Rowdy Saturday-afternoon football games and drunken fraternity men.

A literary tradition as fine as, perhaps finer than, that of any other part of the country.

The near-war needed to enroll James Meredith at Ole Miss.

The Scopes "monkey trial," which created a stereotype of southern attitudes toward educators and education that persists even today in the minds of many of those north of the Mason-Dixon line.

The list could go on and on. But do such images really convey what is happening in the South today in education? Or are they simply relics of a past that existed largely in people's minds anyway? After all, we have been told lately, the South that we used to read about and the South we knew as youngsters is rapidly disappearing; perhaps it's even gone entirely.

There has always been an education gap between the South and the rest of the country. Formal education grew more slowly in the South than elsewhere in the United States, because (according to conventional thinking) the South was largely rural, because as an aristocratically oriented society it wasn't seriously interested in education for the masses, and because the idea of formal schooling for all citizens had fewer champions in Dixie than in New England or the Midwest.

Whether or not one agrees with that interpretation, the fact is that in the early years of this country education was not a top priority in the South. Even though some 260 colleges (half the number of institutions of higher education in the entire nation) were operating in the states of the Old Confederacy when the Civil War broke out, that war effectively dashed whatever educational establishment existed in the South. During the hostilities there was little money for education, and fewer students. Furthermore, schools and college buildings were used for barracks, hospitals, and headquarters. Many were destroyed.

The post–Civil War half century or so brought both high-water marks and low to southern education. An influx of money from philanthropists in the years following the Civil War was responsible for the establishment of many of the region's good private universities (Johns Hopkins, Vanderbilt, and Rice, for example), and for the expansion of others that had been founded earlier as more limited institutions (such as Duke, Emory, and Tulane). That period saw the establishment and enlargement of the first colleges for blacks and the land-grant colleges. But it also was a time of Jim Crow laws and a time when little public money for schools and colleges was available from impoverished states, counties, and cities.

It was not really until after World War II that most southern states began making serious efforts to catch up to the rest of the United States in education. New schools were built, states began to organize their colleges into coherent systems of higher education, the Southern Regional Education Board was established, and the South—beginning to grow prosperous—started to spend more money on its schools and colleges.

But old ways die slowly. The tradition in most southern states of providing as little money as possible for public education continued even when the states were not as poor as they once had been, so progress in expanding and upgrading education proceeded slowly. In recent decades the South has finally begun to close the education gap, but doubts remain. How much has really changed? Have developments in the South and its educational system over the past few decades altered those things for which the South's schools were best known? And if so, have they been changed for better or for worse?

For decades, in the minds of most people, schools and colleges in the South differed from those in the rest of the country because they were racially segregated, usually by law; oriented to the rural society they served; and financially undernourished, largely because the South itself was so poor. As a result education in the South was considered to be—and often was—inferior. Today, those characteristics do not necessarily apply. Racial segregation, while it continues, is not demonstrably different from the de facto segregation that exists in cities throughout the rest of the country. So-called de jure segregation, or segregation endorsed by law, once dominant in the South, no longer exists.

The Supreme Court's 1954 *Brown* v. *Board of Education of Topeka* decision set off a shock wave in the South, and its reverberations are still being felt more than a quarter of a century later. For a long time the South resisted the push by the courts and the federal government to desegregate its schools and colleges. And although to some extent that resistance is still there, many communities in the South report considerably less racial segregation in their schools than does the rest of the country.

Still, the seemingly endless legal struggle over desegregation goes on. In the waning days of President Jimmy Carter's administration, for example, the Justice Department and the Department of Education took a number of steps to ensure that that administration would be remembered as being in the post–World War II liberal Democratic tradition. They pressed several new lawsuits aimed at desegregating school systems, and they notified at least six southern states that their state colleges retained illegal vestiges of the old racially segregated dual systems.

The Reagan administration promised a different approach. At his confirmation hearings Terrel H. Bell, appointed President Reagan's secretary of education, told North Carolina's Senator John P. East that under Ronald Reagan there would be a "dramatic change" in the government's attitude toward desegregation of colleges and universities. Mr. Bell added that he hoped the administration could strike a balance between being "too heavy-handed on the one hand" and undermining progress already made toward equalizing educational opportunity on the other. "We have a responsibility to comply with the law and to see that we are good stewards," Mr. Bell told Senator Edward M. Kennedy.[1]

After holding office for just a few weeks, however, Mr. Bell said that his department would not actively press lawsuits for achieving school desegregation through busing. He said, in fact, that while he might not propose a federal law to outlaw such busing, he would not oppose one. Mr. Bell's department then began what he called "cooperative negotiations" over the desegregation of state college systems. In several cases the Department of Education retreated from the demands of earlier national administrations, especially from the insistence of the Carter administration that some popular programs be shifted from predominantly white campuses to predominantly black ones.

In the administration's first eighteen months the federal government settled long-standing disputes with several systems, including those of Kentucky, Louisiana, Missouri, North Carolina, South Carolina, and West Virginia, as a result of what William Bradford Reynolds, the assistant attorney general, called an "imaginative, constructive approach" to negotiating with the states. Mr. Reynolds argued that "racial quotas" do not work and that "race-conscious methods" of achieving desegregation were not supported by the public. (The government did threaten to get tough with

---

1. Bell testimony cited in *The Chronicle of Higher Education*, January 26, 1981.

Alabama and Virginia, however, and Alabama subsequently agreed to revise its desegregation plan.)

Many civil rights groups were outraged. Arguing in federal court, lawyers for the National Association for the Advancement of Colored People said that acceptance of Louisiana's desegregation plan was a "political decision by the administration to abandon the government's historic role of civil-rights enforcement." Joseph L. Rauh, Jr., counsel to the NAACP Legal Defense Fund, said that none of the plans met the criteria established by the Department of Education during the Carter administration.

The Reagan administration's most explosive action by far in the area of civil rights and education was its announcement in January 1982 that the Internal Revenue Service would no longer deny tax exemptions to schools or colleges simply because they discriminated on the basis of race. Reversing an eleven-year-old policy that had begun during Richard Nixon's administration, Mr. Reagan said he did not believe that tax laws gave the IRS the authority to deal with such matters. He later proposed that Congress enact legislation barring tax exemptions from institutions that display racial bias.

The response was immediate and angry. Many civil rights advocates argued that existing laws and court decisions supported the position of denying tax exemptions to racially biased organizations. One southern newspaper charged that such a policy amounted to "subsidizing discrimination." The United States Commission on Civil Rights chastised the administration for attempting to wipe out years of progress. And Thomas P. O'Neill, Speaker of the House of Representatives, said, "What this country needs is not more legislation, but the clear and unmistakable commitment of the President of the United States to enforce the law." On the other hand, the operators of private all-white schools that had been established in several southern communities by opponents of desegregation said they were pleased with the new policy. Many of them were irritated, however, when Mr. Reagan, reacting to the storm of protest, called on Congress for a measure to outlaw racial discrimination.

President Reagan's policy may not have had much practical effect, but many southerners felt that it represented at least symbolic support for the opponents of desegregation. It seems obvious that enforcing desegregation is not a top priority for the Reagan administration. And if it is not a top priority for the federal government, it is unlikely to be a high priority in the states and localities that would just as soon forget that their schools are segregated. They would prefer to worry about what they consider to be more serious problems.

The issue of whether school desegregation remains on the South's list of serious problems will continue to be debated for some time. However, it is not exclusively a southern issue any longer. One reason for the similarity in desegregation problems between the North and the South is that the South is rapidly becoming as urban as the rest of the country. Although there are not yet southern cities the size of New York or Chicago (and one doesn't need to drive far on a southern interstate highway to find rural areas that don't seem to have been affected much by the twentieth century), the fact is that the South is now home to some of the nation's most rapidly growing urban areas—Houston, Dallas, Miami, and Atlanta, to name only the most obvious. Preliminary census figures indicate that of the country's largest metropolitan areas, fully half the fastest growing ones are in the South. Fourteen of the twenty largest school systems in the United States are now located in the South.

One recent analysis of the 1980 census figures indicated that in most regions of the country more people are leaving metropolitan areas than are entering them. The South was the one exception to that trend.[2] (I pause here to note that as a native Virginian who has lived nearly half his life in Maryland or Washington, D.C., my "version" of the South includes the border states of Maryland, Kentucky, and Missouri, plus the District of Columbia, in addition to the Old Confederacy.)

Urbanization and industrialization in the South may be controversial, but there is little question that they are linked to the region's prosperity. The South is no longer the nation's poor cousin; though it still lags in per capita income, its relative poverty is not as noticeable as in previous dec-

---

2. "Population Trends in Metropolitan Areas," U. S. Bureau of the Census, 1981.

ades. That fact is reflected in the amount of money spent on education. Per-pupil expenditures for education are less than the national average in most southern states, but not by the large margins of past decades. And, in terms of effort, most southern states get good grades. When direct expenditures of state and local funds for education are taken as a percentage of per capita income, about half the southern states performed better than the national average in 1976–77, the most recent year for which figures are available. Of course, when calculations are made on gross totals only, the majority of southern states rank near the bottom.

By some other financial barometers, southern institutions do reasonably well. Thirty-one of the top one hundred colleges and universities that receive funds from the federal government are in the South. Seven of the top twenty states whose percentage of funds for higher education has increased the most over the past ten years are in the South. Four of the ten states whose appropriations for higher education per student have increased the most are in the South.

Two of the top ten and twenty-two of the one hundred best-endowed colleges and universities are in the South. Southern institutions appear to be improving their private fundraising, too. Although only four of the top twenty colleges and universities that raised the most money in 1980 were in the South, two of the largest gifts in the history of American philanthropy have gone to southern universities in the past few years.[3]

Twenty-five percent of the members of the Association of Research Libraries are located in the South. Predictably, in total number of volumes in their holdings, southern institutions don't fare too well; only the University of Texas at Austin is in the top ten. And in acquisitions, libraries in the South are only a bit better (three in the top twenty-five). But five of the leading ten libraries in holdings of microforms are located in the region, reflecting some of the newness of growth at many southern institutions.

Some of these figures represent significant gains for the South relative to

3. One hundred five million dollars, donated to Emory University by Emily and Ernest Woodruff Rund in 1980, cited in *Giving in America* (New York: Conference Board, 1981); $50 million, donated to the University of Richmond in 1969 by E. Claiborne Robins, cited in *The Chronicle of Higher Education*, July 14, 1969.

the rest of the nation. In 1901, for example, when eighteen universities in the nation had endowments of $1.5 million or more, none were in the South; of the thirty having $1 million endowments, only two—Tulane and Vanderbilt—were in the South. In that year southern universities and colleges had less than 9 percent of the total educational endowed funds in the nation and less than 15 percent of the books in the nation's college libraries. According to historian C. Vann Woodward, "The total available annual income for the sixty-six colleges and universities of Virginia, North Carolina, South Carolina, Georgia, Alabama, Mississippi, and Arkansas was $65,843 less than that of Harvard in 1901."[4]

But what about quality? Does the infusion of more money to schools and colleges and more attention to education automatically mean better education? That is a difficult question to answer: not only is quality in education hard to measure, but its very definition can be quite subjective. In a few areas that may relate at least tangentially to quality, however, the South does not fare well.

In the National Assessment of Educational Progress—tests of knowledge in various areas administered nationwide to children at different ages—the South's youngsters uniformly scored lower than those of all the other regions, at all ages, and in all subjects. Since such test scores often reflect family income, the South's continuing low per capita income, despite recent gains and Sunbelt publicity, may explain this lag in test scores. The latest report from the assessment, on a decade's worth of writing tests, does offer some solace for the South, however. "Students from the Southeastern states," it says, "improved from assessment to assessment," with the result that their percentage of papers in the "marginal or better" categories no longer differs statistically from the nation's.[5]

In a recent survey by Standard & Poor of the colleges attended by some 55,000 business executives listed in their directories, no southern institu-

4. C. Vann Woodward, *Origins of the New South, 1877–1913* (Baton Rouge: Louisiana State University Press, 1971), pp. 437–38.

5. "Writing Achievement, 1969–79," National Assessment of Educational Progress, Education Commission of the States, 1981.

tions were among the top twenty-five.[6] In a 1977 survey, two sociologists asked college faculty members to rank departments in nineteen academic fields. Only eight southern institutions were mentioned, only three more than once: the University of North Carolina ranked eleventh in English, tenth in languages, eighth in mathematics, and seventh in sociology; Johns Hopkins ranked fourth in medicine, eighth in English, and tenth in history; the University of Texas at Austin ranked seventh in business and sixth in languages. Other institutions mentioned were North Carolina State, Duke, Texas A&M, Washington (St. Louis), and Virginia.[7]

In a 1969 survey of graduate deans and scholars who were asked to rate graduate departments in thirty-six academic disciplines (published in 1971 by the American Council on Education), only fourteen southern institutions were considered to have at least one "distinguished" department. They were Johns Hopkins and the University of Texas at Austin, twenty-two departments each; Duke, thirteen departments; the University of North Carolina, eleven departments; Washington University (St. Louis), nine; Rice, four; the universities of Florida and Virginia, three each; Maryland and Vanderbilt, two each; and Emory, Florida State, Georgia, and North Carolina State, one each.

Only 37 of the 162 colleges reporting that more than half of their graduates go on to graduate and professional schools are in the South. Of the 203 colleges reporting that more than 75 percent of their students stay to graduate, 47 are located in the South.

If tough admissions standards mean that an institution is of high quality, one might note the following statistics. Only two of the twenty-one U.S. colleges that consider themselves the "most difficult" to get into are in the South—Johns Hopkins and Rice. Only four of the twenty-one institutions where 75 percent of the entering students scored over 600 on the mathematics portion of the Scholastic Aptitude Test are in the South—

6. Survey of Standard & Poor's Corporation, cited in *The Chronicle of Higher Education*, September 29, 1980.

7. Survey by Everett C. Ladd, Jr., and Seymour Martin Lipset, cited in *The Chronicle of Higher Education*, January 15, 1979.

Duke, Johns Hopkins, the U.S. Naval Academy, and Rice. Only one of the seven institutions where 75 percent of the entering students scored over 600 on the verbal portion of the SAT is in the South—New College of the University of South Florida. And none of the five institutions that accept fewer than 20 percent of those who apply is in the South.

Beyond the data, however, lie peoples' perceptions. Not long ago, for example, I had a conversation with a distinguished man in public life who asked me where my son was considering going to college. I responded that he had narrowed his preferences to three or four schools, all in the Northeast. When I added that I hadn't had much luck in interesting my son in schools in the South, he said, "Well, that's just as well. With the exception of a very few schools, they just don't seem to take education very seriously down there."

Many southern educators say that such unintended prejudice is widespread. They cite, for instance, what they consider the "regional bias" of the *New York Times Selective Guide to Colleges*, first published in early 1982. Although 68 of the 225 institutions listed in the book were located in the South, many southerners were quick to point out that descriptions of the quality of education at many southern institutions did not compare favorably with the generally more glowing comments on northeastern colleges. And such disparaging conceptions do not take into account the increasing ability of southern universities to attract highly talented students. Eight of the twenty universities that enrolled the largest numbers of National Merit Scholars were located in the South in the academic year 1982–83, and in total National Merit Scholars Rice University was third nationally, behind only Harvard and Princeton universities. Even without the benefit of campus-supported scholars, Rice (with 241) trailed only Harvard, Princeton, Yale, MIT, and Stanford to rank sixth. When campus-supported National Merit Scholars were included, Rice, Texas A&M, the University of Texas, and Georgia Tech all ranked in the top ten. Such recognition of academic quality is another indication that the South is narrowing the education gap between itself and the rest of the nation.

Many southerners are aware that public secondary school education does not measure up. In large part, of course, this reflects a low level of public support. A recent airplane seatmate of mine, a displaced border-state southerner who now operates a restaurant in Louisiana, told me, "I don't have a family right now, but if and when I do, I guess I'll have to send my kids to private schools." He told how he regularly hires local high-school students to work at his restaurant, and how an astonishingly large percentage of them are unable to read directions or write simple sentences. And a student at Tulane University who tutors in the New Orleans public schools tells of similar shortcomings: students who are unable to handle algebra and geometry because they don't know elementary arithmetic. The fashionable "solution" is to send one's children to private schools, not to work for higher taxes that might allow the improvement of public education.

On the other hand, the statistical evidence that is available seems to indicate that the South is closing one elementary part of the education gap dramatically. In 1950, 3.3 percent of the entire population of the United States over the age of fourteen was illiterate. The corresponding figure for the South was more than 5 percent. By 1970 the illiteracy rate in the nation had shrunk to 1.2 percent, and in the South to less than 2 percent. The difference was halved in two decades.

In higher education, once one gets past that small number of northern institutions that by virtue of history, tradition, and money tend to dominate certain fields—the Ivy League institutions, Chicago, Berkeley, Michigan, and Stanford, for example—southern colleges and universities are now able to hold their own. Some southern universities once had great difficulty keeping good faculty members. When a young professor had acquired a good scholarly track record, he or she was frequently spirited off to the West Coast or Boston or New York with the promise of high salary, unlimited research funds, and fewer students to teach. As recently as 1974, average college faculty salaries in the South were some 16 percent lower than the national average. But six years later, that margin had shrunk to 7 percent. The South's generally lower cost of living may in effect have more than closed the gap. Further, some of the other perquisites that lured teachers away have become harder to find as all institutions of higher education have had to tighten their belts.

Success in keeping scholars is not due entirely to default by northern institutions. Some southern universities have established centers of excellence in certain fields and now have the capacity for doing sophisticated research that they didn't have in past decades. Many of them now have the money and the dedication needed to attract top academic researchers. The University of Texas at Austin, for example, has become the home of the United States Institute for Fusion Studies because of some very aggressive grantsmanship. The university outbid several other institutions, including Yale, Princeton, MIT, and UCLA, for the $1 million a year grant, largely because it was able to persuade one of the nation's leading nuclear scientists to join its faculty. It also offered to match federal funds available for the project dollar for dollar and to double the number of tenured faculty positions that its rivals offered to provide. Another example of the South's new sophistication in attracting academic talent is North Carolina's Research Triangle, which includes academic and commercial scientific research enterprises and now also serves as home for the National Humanities Center.

One cannot seriously discuss southern education without mentioning the plight of the traditionally black colleges. Here is a group of colleges that historically have provided higher education for most of the nation's black college graduates. The alumni rolls of black colleges are a Who's Who of Black America. Over decades of segregation they struggled in almost indescribable poverty to provide the "preachers and teachers" and other professionals needed by the South's black community. Then, with the advent of desegregation and affirmative action, black colleges found their students, their faculty members, their athletes, and even their administrators being wooed by formerly all-white colleges and universities.

Black colleges have been roundly criticized by some scholars and educators for providing an inferior education, and they have even found themselves in trouble with state and federal officials who have been trying to desegregate state college systems. Even faced with all those difficulties, black colleges refused to be integrated out of existence. Today, more than one-fourth of the country's black students are still enrolled in traditionally black colleges. And the colleges are making serious efforts to improve their physical plants, to adjust to changed circumstances, and to respond, as one president put it, to "the dilemma of integration. Promote it we must, but not to our educational and psychological detriment."

Black colleges have mounted a vigorous campaign to persuade the Reagan administration not to reduce federal support for their institutions despite the huge overall cuts in federal funds for education. Spokesmen for the colleges have issued statements to the president's advisers outlining the importance of black colleges and warning of "consequences to the broader society" if federal support is not increased. A proposed "course of action" written by the National Association for Equal Opportunity in Higher Education called for an increase in federal financing for black colleges from $400 million to $900 million over a four-year period. The association also recommended that the government rely on black colleges as centers for "human resource development" that would help upgrade the status of blacks and other minority groups.[8]

While the association's recommendations have not been totally and uncritically accepted in Washington, we must point out that federal funds for black colleges have not been subjected to the kinds of massive cuts that have gutted some other aid-to-education programs. Further, President Reagan issued an executive order in September 1981 directing federal agencies to find ways to provide additional federal support for black colleges and universities.

On some occasions, at least, the order seems to be having some effect. For example, when Meharry Medical College was threatened with loss of accreditation, largely because of financial problems, the Department of Health and Human Services stepped in with $30 million in aid and offered to let the college use the facilities of a nearby veterans' hospital. Meharry, located in Nashville, trained more than 40 percent of all black physicians in the country, according to government statistics.[9]

What does the future hold for southern schools and colleges? Will the

8. "Course of Action," National Association for Equal Opportunity in Higher Education, cited in *The Chronicle of Higher Education*, January 19, 1981.

9. U. S. Department of Health and Human Services data, cited in *The Chronicle of Higher Education*, November 17, 1982.

South's prosperity continue to grow and will the prosperous Sunbelt replace poor old Dixie? Most projections take into account the migration of
Americans to the sunnier climes of the South and West. Indeed, com-
paratively, the South is likely to fare quite well in the decade or two ahead.
That is, school and college enrollments are likely to fall less in the South
than in the rest of the country. Teaching jobs may be less hard to find in
the South than elsewhere. For example, in 1989 the number of high-school
graduates in the entire United States will be 13 percent less than in 1979. In
the Southeast and southcentral region the decline will be only 4 percent.
In 1995 the number of high-school graduates in the United States will be 22
percent less than in 1979. In the South the decline will be only 7 percent.
The eighteen- to twenty-four-year-old population, the traditional age for
most college students, will increase only 0.8 percent in the decade from
1975 to 1985 in the entire nation. In the South, it will increase 3.1 percent.

A new report from the Southern Regional Education Board indicates
that the demand for elementary and secondary school teachers, slow in recent years, may pick up in the 1980s. Already, the report says, teachers are
in short supply in some specialties, including mathematics. Demand for
college teachers will slow in the coming decade. In 1977 the South needed
8,800 new faculty members to replace those departing and to handle additional new students. By 1985 a total of only about 3,600 new faculty members a year will be needed, in all likelihood. But that is still not a real decline. College enrollment in the entire country rose 5.8 percent between
1976 and 1981 and is expected to decline 5.2 percent between 1981 and 1986.
In the South, it increased 7.7 percent by 1981 and will decline only 3.2 percent by 1986. Still, the picture is not entirely rosy. Part-time students, for
instance, are expected to account for a large portion of the new students in
the 1980s as large numbers of women and older people return to college.
When the enrollment figures cited above are translated into the equivalent
of full-time students, the South will have a 3.4 percent increase from 1976
to 1981, followed by a 5.2 percent decrease in the following five years.

That is especially bad news for private colleges and universities, which so
far have not been very successful in attracting part-time students. Most
prognosticators seem to think that research universities will do reasonably

well over the next decade or so but that private liberal arts colleges, especially the smaller ones, may be hit hard by the expected decline in students. Of course, if the Reagan administration's major cutbacks in federal aid-to-education programs should continue, that will complicate matters further. Winfred Godwin, president of the Southern Regional Education Board, has warned:

> The halo of Sunbelt growth should not lead us to avoid consideration of declining enrollments. . . . Our states have made good progress in stabilizing growth through developing more specific roles and missions for institutions, carefully scrutinizing new program proposals, and reviewing existing programs for unnecessary duplication and low quality. Now, these activities need to be carried further to consider the issues of possible reduction, reorganization, merger, and closure.

That assessment may sound grim. But while southern education may be hard-pressed in the coming years, there is both consolation and a bit of irony: the rest of the country will be in worse straits. The South, which has for so long lagged behind in almost all regional comparisons, now has the opportunity to close some of those long-term gaps between itself and the national averages. Nevertheless, in an era when old-fashioned states' rights are in vogue and taxpayers' revolts and efforts to limit government spending abound, it will take great strength of will and political courage to do it.

On Jordan's Stormy Banks
Religion in a Changing South

WILMER C. FIELDS

American religious life has generally been more concerned with fruits than with roots. It has tended to emphasize freedom and the importance of the individual instead of authority and institutionalism. It has valued the active over the contemplative. It has also been characterized by dogmatic rigidity and emotional extravagance. A national religious pluralism has developed that has been often trivial, seldom uniform, never without petty self-interest, strongly parochial, occasionally fanatical, but sometimes prophetic, and almost always dynamic.

In the South the character of the region is embedded in the nature of the churches. With urbanization proceeding somewhat slower here than in other areas of the nation, at least in the past, ruralisms and traditional manners have continued in religious life long after they have disappeared from other sections. Outside of urban areas, religious observances are often festivals of social interchange, emotional outlets that people in cities more often find through other, more secular means. But sectionalism is growing less distinct in religious faith, as in social class and family style. Neither the South nor the nation is what it was in 1940. We have moved through the last forty-odd years as if through a millennium. In an age of diminishing regional identity, the states in the southeastern quadrant of the country are moving away from their agrarianism even as they are slowly losing the southern drawl. There is still in the territory, however, a common mind and spirit, a subconscious memory that the region has lived through a century of extraordinary adversity. Southerners, perhaps more than other Americans, have perceived human nature as frail and inconstant. This, too, is a part of the baggage we take along toward the future.

Society in the South is no longer dominated by religion. It is difficult to pinpoint a time or place when this shift occurred, but it has happened. Many of those who still gravitate to religious institutions have only superficial ties. The business and "busyness" of churches in the United States are generally such that a British visitor was led to say, "One is sometimes left wondering by which of the five entrances God enters into the picture." In the states of the Confederacy, the Baptists (the Southern Baptist Convention and others) have a commanding lead of more than twenty thousand churches. The United Methodists follow next with roughly eight thousand. In these states the combined total of the two denominations accounts for 50 to 90 percent of the church population. There are approximately twenty-two hundred Roman Catholic churches in the same area. Vigorous churches of other denominations are now challenging this traditional strength.

Religion and Culture

The religious dimensions of southern culture and the cultural dimensions of southern religion are two sides of the same coin. The religious phenomena of the South are partly products of the circumstances of southern geography, social composition and mobility, political development, and economic resources. Southern religion is pluralistic, voluntaristic, individualistic, democratic, pragmatic, revivalistic, activistic, and enthusiastic. But even with all of the paraphernalia of southern culture slowing it down, true religion has produced in the South ideas and motivations that have frequently led people to break through the barriers of custom, often at great personal sacrifice, in quest of the will of God. One of the transformations now under way among churches everywhere is a change in what is considered successful. One of the gravest threats to "true religion and undefiled" in the South is this syncretic, tribal, native religion in general, an amorphous religiosity that is subtle, pervasive, and virulent. Our regional history has partly been wrapped up in this folk faith. Its affluence in recent years has given us deceptive assurance that we are on the road to progress, but the truth may be that the churches have simply been well paid for their conformity. An essentially alien social order may have trapped and tamed the churches.

Church and synagogue rites and rituals may be more accurately regarded as the incidentals, not the essentials, of religious life. It is relatively easy for tribal customs, styles, taboos, and practices to get mixed into religious affairs and to become indistinguishable from the vital elements of faith. To see America really at worship today, take a seat in the grandstand for a baseball or football game.

Religion represents and proclaims that which is timeless, but for that very reason it must be timely. Old institutions can easily become bogged down in ancient habits originally formed to meet passing problems. Churches and synagogues must make some kind of accommodation to the world, but it is the accommodation of relevance. In adapting, they free themselves from the walls of their own buildings. In the byways and hedges, among the alleyways and skyscrapers, there is counterfeit religion that needs replacing with the real thing. Over the Southland there is much self-reliance posing as faith, shrewdness labeled as wisdom, anthropology called ethics, and conscience construed to be God. Religion in the South has often suffered from the tendency to become an end in itself, to become self-seeking, self-indulgent, and parochial. It has frequently done more to canonize prejudice than to wrestle for truth, to solidify and petrify the sacred than to redeem and sanctify the secular.

Abraham Joshua Heschel said that religion has become an impersonal affair, an institutional loyalty. It survives on the level of activity rather than in the stillness of commitment. It has fallen victim to the belief that the only things that are real are the ones that we can measure by fact-finding surveys. The only acts that count are the ones people do publicly rather than what they do in private. The chief virtue of religion is social affiliation, rather than conviction. The spirit has become a myth. People treat themselves as if they were created in the likeness of a machine rather than in the likeness of God. As they always have, people today embody the duality of mysterious grandeur and pompous dust. The new factor confronting organized religion in the United States is the need to understand and cope with the outrageous presumption of modern man. The same challenge faces the entire religious enterprise in the Deep South.

Rural Decline

In 1790 Thomas Gray described the mood of rural life in "Elegy Written in a Country Churchyard." The church at Stoke Poges in England still stands, "far from the madding crowd's ignoble strife." Beside the brick building is the cemetery "where heaves the turf in many a mould'ring heap." All about are the elm and yew trees. That scene of peace and quiet makes us feel nostalgia for rural church life. Across America, and particularly in the South, small rural fellowships added great spiritual dimensions to frontier life and afforded strength to the sturdy settlers. Even today, rural churches make up about 70 percent of the 36,000 churches affiliated with the Southern Baptist Convention. They have about one-third of the gifts. But with the general decline in rural population, these churches face serious problems. The automobile is both boon and bane to the existence of the country church. In many places it is the one mechanism that holds the organization together. In other places it has helped rural churches develop dynamic programs. But either way, it has been a major factor in the turnover in population that has affected all of the churches in the South. Rural churches have been depleted in great numbers.

Factors Affecting the Churches

Churches in the South are changing. Some are in rapid transformation. Some are in slow metamorphosis. Some are growing, some are declining, but all are moving. One of the factors that is modifying the churches is this very process of questioning, of self-examination, of criticism. Alterations and permutations in the life of the church rest on the proposition that truth, like knowledge, has nothing to fear from ruthless examination. Error does. If the biblical estimate of the origin, nature, and destiny of the human population is indeed what we assert it to be, then our witness to it in the 1980s will be the stronger because of honest and thorough examination. Erich Fromm and others have shown that dogmatism is basically an immature form of religion. The unenlightened and the insecure shun inquiry, no less than do the prejudiced and the fearful. Intelligent self-criticism is one mark of maturity. The evaluative process itself is opening southern church windows to admit fresh air.

Another factor shaking up churches these days is the shift of society to a secular mode. Today, far more than in Emerson's day, "Things are in the saddle and ride mankind." Materialism reigns. Market day is judgment day. Even people themselves are commodities with value. More and more their security lies in conformity, in never being more than two feet away from the herd. The first line of Harvey Cox's book, *The Secular City*, reads, "The rise of urban civilization and the collapse of traditional religion are the two main hallmarks of our era and are closely related movements."[1] "Traditional" religion has not exactly fallen apart, but those of us who are deeply engaged in it have an uneasy feeling that Harvey Cox and others like him may know something that we don't know.

The gauges that we hold up to the wind these days are not at all reassuring. The automatic evolution toward bigger and better things, which we came to expect in southern religion in the 1940s and 1950s, is long gone. There has been a decided change in recent years in the way people understand their lives together. Whatever vocabulary they use to express it, people today seem to sense that they have been left with the world on their hands; they can no longer blame fortune or the furies for what they do with it. Dietrich Bonhoeffer called this awakening "man's coming of age."[2]

Rapid urbanization in the South these days means a new level of imper-

1. Harvey Cox, *The Secular City* (New York: Macmillan, 1965).
2. *Ethics* (New York: Macmillan, 1959).

sonality, tolerance, and anonymity. It also means a richer store of perspectives. It brings with it new gods, new values and belief systems. Cox says, "If secularization designates the content of man's coming age, urbanization describes the context in which it is occurring."[3] A typhoon of secularity is rolling over Dixieland. The era that is sweeping upon us is already looking beyond the religious rules and rituals of the past for its meanings and morality. Religion in the Bible Belt may indeed be reduced eventually to the role of a hobby, a regional or ethnic identification, or just another among many aesthetic delights. If such an era is upon us, then we will do well to heed Bonhoeffer's advice to learn to speak of biblical concepts in secular language, to speak of God in a fashion that secular people will hear and understand.

An additional influence affecting the church is government. The sad, ironic fact is that all too often politicians have had to prod southern church people into doing something about our public responsibilities. City ordinances, state laws, and federal legislation have dragged us kicking to our posts of civic duty. Measures affecting racial justice, civil rights, welfare, education, health, the problems of old age, crime prevention, highway safety, and the minimum wage, to mention a few, have been debated and enacted with all too little religious or theological evaluation. Now when people are in trouble, they turn to the government, not to the church. The role of the state is expanding, while that of the church in many places is becoming more and more marginal. The man of the moment, especially in the South, is the politician. He is the adjuster, the arbiter, the broker of the many conflicting and competitive interests of our time. He and his colleagues are the movers and shakers of our society. With business and industrial leaders, who are now moving rapidly to the front, the politicians are remolding southern life. They are changing society without the insight or inspiration of dynamic religious forces, and the reason is that we have neglected our responsibilities. If they produce a mechanized, impersonal, homogeneous, overbearing world, it will be because southern religious institutions have failed to keep the individual in focus.

3. *The Secular City*, p. 4.

Still another force that has a bearing on religious life in the South is education. Unfortunately, education has not always been a high enough priority in the region. At one time it was primarily for the planter aristocracy. Education was a means by which the South sought to provide a Renaissance education for an ideal gentleman. The Civil War and its aftermath left the South defenseless but defensive, with a garrison psychology, a shattered economy, and a long list of priorities that often placed education far down the line. Not until after World War II did something like an intellectual rebirth become apparent in the region.

Two key dates mark dramatic changes in the nature of education, including religious education, in southern states as well as in the rest of the nation. The first is May 17, 1954, when the Supreme Court declared in a unanimous decision that "separate but equal" schools for blacks were unconstitutional. The chain of events that this decision set off focused attention on the inadequacies of the entire educational system. The second date is October 4, 1957, when the Soviet Union launched its first satellite, Sputnik I. This achievement jarred the entire western world into realizing that the U.S.S.R. was considerably ahead in the sophisticated sciences. Out of this came the most frantic push that education has received in all of American history. Vast government funds soon augmented the nation's uneven educational system. Now church-related colleges and universities must also meet rising standards and skyrocketing costs and must reexamine their role in the total educational effort of the nation. In support of their own colleges and in response to a rising level of education in their membership, the churches must still make many modifications.

There are other factors affecting churches, forcing variations and innovations both now and in the near future. Southern people, for instance, are better educated, more cosmopolitan, more pragmatic, more impatient with the old clichés, less impressed with the preening and posturing of old-style spellbinders. They want straightforward answers to some elementary questions. Church and synagogue planners have become more goal-oriented, more conscious of long-range planning, more willing to accommodate group effort, and more innovative in their approaches to the many religious challenges. Affluence has provided more funds, giving the churches an opportunity to participate more fully in a wider range of enterprises. A growing sense of social responsibility cannot help but alter the future outreach of religious groups.

Mixed into all of this ferment is an increased consciousness among southerners that good works begin at home. It is a hypocrisy of the worst order to send messengers of enlightenment to other shores and then live like the devil himself here at home. This new sense of integrity about religious commitment is on the horizon—about the size of a man's hand, but growing.

A Changing Role in Mission

The incredible restlessness of forty million people moving around the country each year represents new growth opportunities for thousands of southern churches. This transmigration is making it possible for sedentary, satisfied congregations to become missionary outposts.

At the time of Jesus, the world population was perhaps 250 million. We now have almost that many people in the United States alone. It is becoming clear to spiritual leaders that it is not enough these days just to have beautiful sanctuaries, large educational buildings, clever sermons, and complicated programs. These are really quite incidental to that deep commitment to God and godliness, that essential sense of awe and amazement that is at the heart of the religious experience.

The dislocations of the past forty years have left few relationships untouched. The perpetual motion of people geographically is matched by movement up and down the economic and social scale. Life on all sides has been caught up in unfamiliar problems and without dependable guidelines from the past. A new order is still ascending in the South, keyed to progress, often heedless of history, more affluent and heterogeneous than the order that it supplants. In the swirl, churchmen are facing baffling new complexities. Adjustments, formerly made over long decades, are now required in a few years. New uncertainties have followed on the heels of old ones that faded away. Pathos and anxiety persist, cropping up in surprising forms and places. In the midst of all these threats, southern churches have not always emerged as engines of spiritual and social reconstruction. Our slowness to respond to the racial revolution in the United States is the most flagrant example. We have too often been guided by ideas that are relevant to another generation. We thus do some things that are unnecessary, some that are unwise, and some that are downright irrational.

The work of churches and synagogues today must be related not only to a highly mobile society but also to a highly impermanent society. Each of us becomes acquainted with more people in a year than a feudal serf met in a lifetime. The ties that most people establish today, however, are very tentative and perishable. In this age of transience we are being psychologically conditioned to fewer long-lasting links and more short-term relationships. This new temporariness applies to values and things as well as to people. As we approach a new millennium of the Christian era, human relations are being foreshortened as time is being telescoped. The year A.D. 2000 is rushing toward us. Whatever may lie on the other side of that epochal date, fluctuation will set the tone of our lives until then. We are entering upon mercurial times. The Judaeo-Christian witness to an imperishable faith must be geared to the times or be left behind.

New Difficulties

Tougher times are ahead for religion in the South, as for the nation at large. Budgets are impressive. Membership rolls list millions. Our problem is not trouble from the outside. Rather, the danger comes from blight within, far more insidious than an enemy outside. Our malady may be too much religion and too little faith, and not enough wisdom to know the difference. One of the hazards of our day seems to be the ease with which organized religion can be sidetracked from its central mission. A strong reaction to this bland, hands-off, do-nothing style of religious life rose to prominence in the national elections of 1980. The "religious right" sprang, seemingly full grown, into the nation's politics, toppling candidates on their hit list and boosting the political fortunes of their heroes. This coalition of religious fundamentalism, right-wing politics, one-issue pressure groups, and television preachers held together long enough to accomplish a surprising number of their goals. It remains to be seen, however, whether this kind of concerted action of strident groups like the so-called Moral Majority is a significant new factor in American politics and religion or just a flash in the pan. Coalitions are notoriously difficult to hold together. In its first appearance in the major political leagues, this one mixed some legitimate moral issues with partisan politics, baptized the entire mishmash with religious oratory, and rather frequently spread simplistic theology over its extensive jerry-rigged agenda.

The South is no longer a simple land of catfish and honeysuckle. Whereas the region has given sanctuary to the "religious right" here and there, its religious and political judgments are becoming more like the national pattern. The soundness of that collective judgment will undoubtedly be tested severely over the next few years on church and state constitutional principles and in their application to religion and public affairs.

Too Little, Too Late?

The church is still the South's most pervasive institution. Protestantism reigns supreme in the region, to an extent unmatched in the hemisphere. Outspoken doubters and village atheists have been relatively few. Habits are strong. People are inclined to accept anything that has been around for a long time, and to venerate whatever is old-fashioned and heavily redolent of the past simply because it is old. They set considerable store by putting old customs and practices in new dress, thus protracting the lifespan of cherished minor heresies. With time, and assisted by debate, outdated practices have become increasingly elaborate, have developed a large literature, and have even acquired a mystique. The South has been a collective of local political, cultural, and religious neighborhoods, each a tiny molecule of "the southern way of life." In each, the practice has too often been to placate ancestral spirits by participating in the local rituals, regardless of how outworn they may be.

Traditionally, the South has given its highest regard to law, the ministry, medicine, teaching, and banking; but this veneration is changing. Today chemists, physicists, and engineers are the rising aristocrats among professionals. The new industrialism is strong-minded in its demands and pays little heed to traditions, established patterns of culture, or even history.

Shallow churchmanship, even when billed as "missions" or "ministries," no longer suffices. A congregation of the faithful must be something more than a fellowship of good-natured, well-meaning, and friendly people. A congregation of true believers requires more than chumminess. The renewal that this fast-moving age demands of southern religion is a drastic renewal. Perhaps it is time, to use Shakespeare's phrase, to "unthread the rude eye of rebellion."

This may call for the advocates of a life of faith to take a leaf from the scientists' book. Science, so often vilified and excoriated by churchmen, is a way of looking at the world, an approach to truth. It stresses openmindedness and a willingness to reserve judgment and to adapt. A meaningful renewal of the church in an age of high transience also calls for a change in emphasis from yesterday to tomorrow, from traditional habits to the habit of anticipation. We must explore the religious possibilities of tomorrow as systematically as we now study religious history.

Minorities

The most significant symbol of change in the South is the American black population. Over the past twenty-five years they have made more progress toward true citizenship than in all the rest of the approximately three hundred and fifty years that they have been a part of American life. The dispossessed, the culturally deprived, the social outcasts have often been an embarrassment to church and community. We have despised and rejected them, esteeming them not, and have hidden our faces from them. But in so doing we have rejected the reclaiming and redeeming role of religion. Here is where hope lies for a new and better day for religion in the South, in becoming a more effective agent of change. At no time in American peacetime history have such substantial social adjustments been attempted in so short a period of time as in the past few years. For years to come we will still have before us the problem of maintaining a balance between order and change, and the enlightened conscience must continually be brought to bear on the race issue. To perpetuate a sense of inferiority among any of our neighbors is to be untrue to the spirit of our best religious traditions.

Religious influence in American life is never uniform or simple. It is always subtle, indirect, and sometimes puzzling. In a time of changing demands for mission outreach, we must determine to look up and not down, to look forward and not back, to look out and not in, and to lend a hand.

Urban Man

For a long time there has been a consensus that cities are evil: God made the country; man made the cities. Is a city basically alien to the kingdom of God? Is there a fundamental hostility between the city and the spirit of religion? Babel, Ninevah, Babylon, Tyre, Sidon, Sodom, Gomorrah were all bad! But there was also John's vision of the New Jerusalem, "coming down out of heaven from God." Almost symbolically, the Bible opens with a garden, but it closes with a city. Both are the locales of God at work.

The city rewards success and punishes failure. It has a voracious appetite for talent and enterprise. It is ruthless in its rejections. It tests people, uses them, and rejects them. It is a threat to family, neighborliness, community spirit, and religion. But the city is also a promise. In it, people maintain a slender victory of order over chaos, reason over unreason, law over anarchy, civilization over barbarism. Here people reveal their ultimate vulnerability and dependency. Because the city has greatly enlarged the scope, efficiency, and the outreach of human ability, the question is now whether it can also enhance the life of faith, hope, and love. Harvey Cox says in *The Secular City* that this new phenomenon, metropolis, represents liberation and fulfillment.[4] Whether or not this is so, it is inconsistent for people to love God and neighbor and then hate the neighborhood. We need a sense of continuity, stability, and order. These are created primarily through the responses of family and neighborhood. In the bewilderment of our spreading urbs and suburbs, we grasp for straws of similarity and familiarity. The near-panic for status in some quarters is a symptom of this struggle for identity. The urban life that is now spreading rapidly over the old rural South is profoundly affecting family life.

All citizens of cities tend to be casual visitors, and acquaintance is superficial. The city may be cosmopolitan, but its inhabitants are provincial. In a real sense, each individual is an alien. The city becomes a crucible for freedom or bondage, for creation or destruction. It frees us to go the way of our own choosing, to work out our own victory or defeat. As Pogo said, "We have met the enemy, and they is us." Here in the throbbing cities are the greatest personal and social needs of our age, presenting a fertile place for true believers in the South to express their faith, life, and work. Religion has often abandoned the central part of the cities, leaving their redemption to business and industry. In the opening line of his book, *The Suburban Captivity of the Churches*, Gibson Winter says that the metropolis will be the principal field of religious expansion in the immediate future.[5] We southerners cannot afford to sleep through this revolutionary development in American religious life.

The New Sociology

The big distances between people in the United States today are not geographical but sociological. In the past, southerners have tended to think of the far West, the folks way up north, and especially anyone above the

4. *The Secular City*, p. 47.

5. Gibson Winter, *The Suburban Captivity of the Churches: An Analysis of Protestant Responsibility in the Expanding Metropolis* (Garden City, N. Y.: Doubleday and Co., 1961).

Mason-Dixon Line as rather remote citizens who are generally beyond the pale. Not to be outdone in provincialism, other sections of the country have reciprocated. But time has changed much of that. The forms, institutions, and functions of United States subcultures have been altered rapidly during the past quarter of a century. There is a new cosmopolitan character to southern business, politics, education, communication, and almost every other facet of the associated life of southerners today. For instance, some 400 of the 500 largest corporations in the United States have branch offices in Atlanta. Personnel in such companies come from everywhere. It is common now to find people almost anywhere who have lived in several parts of the nation. The social interaction that this represents is of historic significance in all areas, but especially in the South. As a result, the land of the Old Confederacy is revising its image of itself. The local yokel with bizarre ideas is having more and more trouble staying invincibly provincial.

The South's distinctive values, its habits, its forms of self-congratulation are evolving into a broader American pattern. The region's proper sense of its individuality will continue in some manner for many generations to come. But the South is moving more and more into the nation's mainstream. The real provincialism of the space age is no longer a matter of geography. It is a provincialism that is an ingrown narrowness of mind and heart. It is a defensiveness, an ignorance, a misbegotten sense of separateness, a perversion of collective behavior, and a lack of compassion for the surrounding social order.

With increasing urbanization, Americans can expect great social changes as we approach a new century. Scientific and technological innovations affect the way we shop, the way we relax, and the way we travel. Already, we are literally changing the face of the earth. But this is only part of the story. People are also changing in how they think and feel, how they respond. The age of transience is having its effect on personality, on the inner being, and it is precisely at this point that churches and synagogues can render a relevant ministry. In stable times the functions of society are routine and rather familiar. New kinds of decisions are not required very often. But when society changes as fast as ours is now doing, the problems do not repeat themselves very often. Instead, we must constantly cope with new dilemmas. Too much novelty, too much excitement, too much change tends to undermine one's ability to make rational decisions. People can become glutted with more information and impressions than they can process. Rationality and sanity depend on comprehending one's surroundings. These days, by the time we think that we understand our little corner of the world, it has already changed to something else. This disorientation has profound ethical, moral, social, and, above all, spiritual implications. This speaks of a pervasive need of our times. It is also our great opportunity to proclaim liberation through a religious faith on some of the new frontiers of American life.

The progress of the past twenty years has been phenomenal. The developments of the next twenty years doubtless will eclipse and exceed all of our wildest imaginations. The noblest qualities of human beings certainly do not lie within the realm of the predictable. The historic durability and adaptability of southerners should serve the region well as we move into an exciting era of religious change.

Springtime in the Desert
The Fine Arts and Their Patronage in the Modern South

W. L. TAITTE

In a well-known essay published in 1920, "The Sahara of the Bozart," H. L. Mencken condemned the condition of the arts in the southern United States in absolute terms:

> In all that gargantuan paradise of the fourth-rate there is not a single picture gallery worth going into, or a single orchestra capable of playing the nine symphonies of Beethoven, or a single opera-house, or a single theater devoted to decent plays, or a single public monument (built since the war) that is worth looking at, or a single workshop devoted to the making of beautiful things.

He was willing to grant the region two poets (Robert Loveman and John McClure, however obsure those names are today) and a single prose writer (James Branch Cabell), but no other artists or thinkers:

> When you come to critics, musical composers, painters, sculptors, architects and the like, you will have to give it up, for there is not even a bad one between the Potomac mud-flats and the Gulf. Nor an historian. Nor a sociologist. Nor a philosopher. Nor a theologian.

Nor a scientist. In all these fields the south is an awe-inspiring
blank—a brother to Portugal, Serbia and Esthonia.[1]

Mencken's diatribe against the South shocked many and was taken much
to heart; it has even been given credit in part for the artistic revival that
began to take place in the South in the 1920s.[2]

That revival has continued, so that today things are obviously very different. If nothing else, we have more than enough sociologists, not to
speak of historians. Of writers, too, we have had at least our share. It does
not take regional pride to convince people that William Faulkner is the
best American novelist of the century, and plenty of smaller peaks and
foothills surround that great eminence. We may not be able to boast of
painters, sculptors, or composers of such undisputed greatness. But if it is
not yet settled just how good the good ones are, there are certainly plenty
of bad examples of each species now between the Potomac and the Gulf.

The second half of Mencken's indictment thus no longer rings true at all.
But in reading the first of the excerpts I have quoted, a nagging suspicion
arises. In the South we have a number of orchestras, capable of playing
Beethoven adequately enough even if taxed by composers demanding
more virtuosity of execution. We have several opera companies, though
most of them do not have adequate opera houses. We have plentiful theaters dedicated to plays decent and indecent, though not many with extraordinary standards of performance. It is a moot question whether any
public monument built anywhere in the country since Mencken's diatribe
is worth viewing, but we have our share of those with fervent partisans—
Henry Moore boulders and Alexander Calder or Joan Miró tinkertoys
now grace the plazas of the South as surely as they do Yankee ones. And
we have picture galleries worth going into, although again it is question-
able just how long visitors can sustain their attentions before they get an
unconquerable urge to leave. Mencken could not accuse the modern South

1. H. L. Mencken, "The Sahara of the Bozart," in *Prejudices: A Selection*, ed. James T. Far-
rell (New York: Vintage Books, 1958), p. 71.

2. See Fred C. Hobson, Jr., *Serpent in Eden: H. L. Mencken and the South* (Chapel Hill:
University of North Carolina Press, 1974), pp. 57–79.

of being a paradise of the fourth-rate. But he might allege, in a somewhat smaller voice, that it is a purgatory of the second-rate.

This allegation would in some sense be true, but it would be misleading and even unfair. The artistic phenomena in the first part of Mencken's attack are all corporate rather than individual in nature. A community or a group within a community must build a gallery or a monument, establish an orchestra or an opera company. Also, these institutions are all (in the modern United States, at least) curatorial or museumlike in nature, rather than products of original creative impulses. The general tone of Mencken's essay implies that southerners are uncivilized louts, but that does not follow from the mere absence of institutions such as symphony orchestras and art museums. What this absence mostly implied in 1920—and what the failure of the South to match the best of these in other parts of the country implies in the 1980s—is that the South does not have enough people with enough money gathered together in single places to support such institutions, of any quality in 1920, or of the highest quality today.

Artistic institutions of these kinds require great sums of money, and for the most part the size of the sums means that many people must chip into the pot, both as consumers and as underwriters. The obviousness of such a consideration is, I suppose, implicit in my topic: patronage and the fine arts. You can't have one without the other—at least not the institutional kinds of fine arts. Faulkner could hide away on the edge of town in Oxford, Mississippi, to write. Flannery O'Connor could convalesce on her mother's farm outside Milledgeville, Georgia, far from an urban center. O'Connor actually did receive a little patronage in terms of foundation grants and the like, but that does not blur my point that writing, not being an essentially communal occupation, does not require large communities in order for its practitioners to enter the big time. In the absence of an Esterhazy, though, opera is at a disadvantage out in the country. There are a few Maecenases as rich as Croesus, and they can endow a gallery or hire an orchestra any time and any place they choose. But taxes being what they are, important artistic institutions for the most part presuppose large city populations.

Most of the biggest and richest and most important artistic institutions in the United States date from a decade or two either side of 1900—the period just before Mencken's essay was written. I think it important to note that in 1900 there was within the states that had formed the Confederacy only one of the thirty largest cities in the United States. That was New Orleans, then the twelfth largest city in the country. Even so, New Orleans was not a boom town; it was actually decreasing in relative size, since it had been fifth largest in 1850. This trend continues today, since New Orleans was only the thirty-third largest metropolitan area in 1980. The only other city of any real size in the Old South in 1900 was Memphis. Yet Worcester, Massachusetts, and Patterson, New Jersey, were both larger than Memphis, the second metropolis of the South, not to speak of the much smaller Atlanta or Richmond.[3]

I contend that it is cities, not regions, that should be praised or condemned for their artistic institutions. As a corollary of the principle that it takes a substantial metropolis to produce noteworthy artistic institutions, I suggest that it helps if the metropolis is undergoing substantial growth. Cities with expanding economic resources tend to have more money left over from necessities with which to endow the beautiful things in life, and with which to show off. The only city in the South that Mencken might reasonably have expected to be participating in the institutional artistic life of the nation in 1920 was New Orleans. There were no doubt a number of social and cultural factors, some of them regional in character, that contributed to New Orleans's failure to found a great orchestra or a great museum during the early years of this century. But probably the most critical factor, as well as the most obvious, was that it was not a city of great growth. Considerably smaller than Baltimore or Cincinnati, it was like them declining in relative prominence and power. If one were to point a finger at the New Orleans of 1920, one would in all justice have to criticize those cities, and, more vehemently, St. Louis, which had been the fourth largest city in the country in 1900. I understand that the upriver city is doing pretty well by the arts now, but was it doing so much better than New

3. My population figures are derived from the *1982 World Almanac* (New York: Newspaper Enterprise Association, Inc., 1981), pp. 202–3.

Orleans sixty years ago? The most important artistic product of these cities back then were jazz and the blues, but these were forms of musical expression that did not require expensive patronage. The arts that required large financial outlays were doing badly in the South in 1920 not because the South exhibited any mystical southern backwardness but because, as is well known, the South was rural and poor.

The relative urbanization of the North at the turn of the century still has important consequences for artistic institutions in the South today, and would probably still have these consequences even if southern cities were not still smaller, by and large, than northern cities. Institutions take time to grow and mature. Most especially, audiences take time to acquire the habits of going to musical and dramatic performances. The principal reason that the Atlanta Symphony cannot quite compete with the Boston Symphony in quality is that Boston pays its musicians 53 percent more per year than Atlanta does. It also employs fully sixteen more players for its orchestra.[4] At the root of these differences is money. In theory nothing keeps the Atlanta Symphony board from going out to raise each year the $1.2 million it would require to make up the annual discrepancy in musicians' salaries, but in practice things seldom happen that way. Budgets grow because the habits of patronage grow—both in attendance and in contribution—and these tend to grow gradually. So not only does Atlanta still have only about half the population of Boston in its metropolitan area—and sheer numbers mean very much in this area of patronage—but it is also playing an eternal game of catch-up with cities that have had a head start.

Art museums are even more heavily handicapped by the mere fact of not having been around sixty or eighty or a hundred years ago. A 1975 report by the National Endowment for the Arts showed that of the largest museums—those with yearly budgets of a million dollars or more—39 percent were founded before 1900 and fully 74 percent before 1920.[5] These

4. "Wage Scales and Conditions in the Symphony Orchestras, 1979–1980 Season: Section A," American Federation of Musicians pamphlet, 1980.

5. *Museums USA: A Survey Report* (National Research Center of the Arts, 1975), p. 5.

figures cast light on another aspect of the report; although there are actually more museums in the southeastern United States than in the Northeast (18 percent versus 17 percent), the Northeast has 40 percent of the major museums in the country and the Southeast only 5 percent.[6] Museums also grow gradually, and those of the South obviously have not even begun to catch up. Sadly, there seems to be no realistic hope that they ever will.

I make this rather alarming statement because of the conditions that now prevail in the odd world of the buying and selling of major artworks. The laws that many countries have passed in recent decades limiting the export of works of art and the enormous inflation in the prices of paintings and sculpture mean that it would be nearly impossible to assemble today the sorts of collections that our great museums have. Only a handful of cities in the world have museums with holdings to compare with the five or six greatest museums in the United States—and most of those are centered around the greatest artists of their own countries. Napoleon acquired many of the treasures of the Louvre through military conquest. Our own robber-baron art collectors at the end of the nineteenth century used economic rather than military power, and hardly anybody has enough economic power to achieve the same ends today. If the extraordinary paintings and other pieces assembled, say, in New York's Frick Collection were to be put on sale today (one at a time, so as not to alarm the market too drastically), they might bring, in my rather crude calculations, something like a half-billion to a billion dollars. And the Frick's exquisite collection is a small one; I say nothing of what the collection of the Metropolitan Museum of Art up the street might bring. A museum in Fort Worth, Texas, the Kimbell, has often been compared to the Frick. The Kimbell has spent prodigious amounts of money and acquired many lovely pieces in the few years of its existence. It bought a very handsome major Rembrandt several years ago, but this was one of its two or three most expensive purchases. Such acquisitions will not be made very often. The Frick, on the other hand, has three or four choice Rembrandts and three of only a few dozen Vermeers in the world. Neither the Kimbell, one of the richest southern

6. Ibid., p. 17.

museums, nor any other that I know about has the financial resources to acquire today works of the quality and quantity of those of the Frick—not to speak of the Metropolitan—even if those works were available. And they are not available, at least not in the quantity that could produce truly major museums in every principal southern city. Institutions such as the Kimbell and the Ringling Museum in Sarasota, Florida, will remain both more limited than northern museums in scope and isolated in their hard-won achievements. Even truly magnificent private collections such as those of the Menil family in Houston, soon to be housed in a major new museum, cannot match in coverage the great collections gathered in the nineteenth century.

This peculiar situation of a very limited set of masterpieces anywhere in the world, most of which are already safely in museums and jealously guarded, mercifully exists only in the field of older works of visual art. The prospects of the other institutional arts in the South are much less grim. Even in the visual arts, southern museums and galleries have been holding their own in acquiring more recent (and more plentiful) pictures and statues. The number of art galleries of the sort that sell, rather than simply exhibit, works of art has in fact become prodigious—although whether the phenomenon is more an artistic than an economic one is hard to say. Southern architecture has joined the mainstream of American practice, for better and for worse. And in the performing arts we have experienced a Renaissance since World War II, and especially since 1960, comparable to the southern literary Renaissance in the 1920s.

The states of the Old Confederacy now have six of the thirty-one orchestras classified as major by the American Symphony Orchestra League. There are also nine orchestras classified as regional and twenty-one as metropolitan, levels at which performances are often very solid and enjoyable. Theatrical activity is similarly burgeoning. Eight of the fifty-four members of the League of Resident Theatres are in the South, but this is merely the tip of the iceberg of professional and near-professional dramatic production. Even a city as small as Anniston, Alabama (population approximately 30,000), can boast a resident and touring theater company in the Alabama Shakespeare Festival, officially sponsored by the state. All of these theaters are following in the footsteps of the older resident professional companies, the senior of which is Houston's Alley Theatre, founded in 1947. Dance companies are not so numerous but are coming along nicely.

Perhaps the most impressive of all the statistics is the proliferation of opera companies in the South. Sixteen of the sixty or so American opera companies are now in the southern states. The Greater Miami Opera Association has launched some important productions, and the Virginia Opera Assocation of Norfolk has given American premieres of several important pieces; but the most notable southern opera companies are in Houston and Dallas. The Houston Grand Opera celebrated its twenty-fifth season in 1981; the Dallas Civic Opera passed a similar landmark in 1982. The Dallas company has had productions that rivaled those anywhere in the world from the start; Houston has achieved such standards only in the last seven or eight years. It seems remarkable to me that two such companies can exist in one of our southern states, purveying a performing art generally considered the most abstruse of all and certainly the most expensive of all. Since the standards of each company, production for production, match those of any company anywhere, they can fall behind others only in terms of quantity, and now the Houston Grand Opera must be ranked by that standard as at least fifth in the nation, after the two New York companies, Chicago, and San Francisco. These are only two out of the many examples of artistic sectors where southern cities actually outperform rather than fall short of their numerical rank of population within metropolitan areas. (Houston, for instance, is only the tenth largest metropolitan area.)

Thus I think there can be no question that the southern urban areas are now at least holding their own in the arts. But the question still arises whether there is any meaning in lumping southern cities together as a group. In the southern literary Renaissance some writers adamantly presented themselves precisely as southerners—as, for example, the Fugitives. Critics persistently found categories of a regional nature in which to put many of the others. But no symphony orchestra was ever praised or castigated for being Southern Gothic. Institutions dedicated to displaying Rembrandt or performing Beethoven or Shakespeare would find it hard to take on a regional identity even if they tried. In fact, the more thoroughly professional any of the performing arts institutions is, the less likely either the management or the performers are to come from anywhere in particular, including the southern regions that give them a home. This is especially true in music, where the managers of the large institutions tend to be from the mobile international set. Opera singers are on a circuit and come and go, and orchestral players must audition behind a screen and can hail from anywhere. The musical forms that do have significant regional roots tend to be popular in nature and do not fall within the dueling ground marked off by Mencken; I refer, of course, to country music as well as to jazz and the blues (and the latter two have even been nationalized and deprived of much of their regional character over the years).

Theaters tend to be more deeply rooted than the institutions serving up classical music. Often they have been founded by a native of the locale, and at last it is possible to make something of a career, though not a very lucrative one, as an actor in the larger southern cities. Visual artists too are finding it possible to build a reputation and make a living while staying at home. A number of art critics have been arguing that it may actually be an artistic advantage these days to be "in the provinces," so to speak—not to be in New York or in the other centers of fashion, so as not to be caught up in the tides of trivial modishness that have been damaging art. But I have not heard that any significant regional style has developed that would set the South or any part of it off in the way that the literary movements of the 1920s and later periods did.

Nor has there been a musical or dramatic regionalism of any importance. Tennessee Williams is identifiably southern, and has spawned many imitators but not a coherent school of drama. Although he worked with Margo Jones in Dallas early in his career, his oeuvre has grown up independent of any particular theater company; wherever the plays have opened, they were always written with an eye on Broadway. Jones's early death, however, did not keep Dallas from becoming the most prolific mother of playwrights in the South. The Dallas Theater Center—for most of its history essentially a drama school with a journeyman program and a large number of resident artist-teachers rather than an Equity professional theater—has developed a group of playwrights in permanent residence, many of whom write on regional themes. One of these, the late Preston Jones, is the most important playwriting figure to come out of the American regional theater movement; but his recent premature death destroyed hope in many that the rather eccentric organization of the Theater Center would eventually justify itself through the creative products of those it shelters. Dallas has produced many other playwrights, including D. L. Coburn (winner of the 1978 Pulitzer Prize) and Southern Methodist University drama school graduates Jack Heifner, James McLure, and Beth Henley (winner of the 1981 Pulitzer Prize). Ironically, though the work of these playwrights gained recognition through small, mostly regional theaters, these theaters were a long way from Dallas, most notably in Louisville, Kentucky. A lot of artistic activity, both in production and creation, is occurring in cities like Dallas, but even in a single city the strands are too diverse to allow for easy generalization. This is even truer of a broad region like the South as a whole.

I can see little evidence that the cities of the South today share any regional characteristics except that they are smaller and newer than those of the Northeast and Midwest. The cities of the Old Confederacy share this set of circumstances with those of the Southwest, and it seems to me that the "Sunbelt" label tells essential truths about what is going on in the artistic growth and the present status of the arts in the cities of the southern United States, east or west. George Brown Tindall in *The Emergence of the New South, 1913–1945* noted how closely the idea of a New South was tied to the economic growth and urbanization of the region. He observed that five of the seven fastest-growing metropolitan areas in the nation in the 1920s were in the South: Miami, Dallas, Houston, Tulsa, and Oklahoma City.[7] Interestingly, the other two were Los Angeles and San Diego. All seven were in Florida, Texas, Oklahoma, and California—the Sunbelt in embryo. The Jim Crow laws no doubt set apart the states of the South proper from the other states along the southern tier of the country be-

7. George Brown Tindall, *The Emergence of the New South, 1913–1945, A History of the American South*, Volume 10, ed. Wendell Holmes Stephenson and E. Merton Coulter (Baton Rouge: Louisiana State University Press, 1967), p. 95.

tween 1920 and 1960. But since the death of the segregation laws, it has been increasingly hard to tell the two areas apart, in statistics that have to do with the arts as well as in other statistics.

Compare, for instance, Miami and San Diego. Along with Tampa, they are the only two cities in the country that have National Football League franchises but not major symphony orchestras. Both Miami and San Diego, however, have two of the most important smaller opera companies in the country. I do not wish to make too much of fortuitous symmetries, but there is another pleasing parallel between east and west in that two of the most important summer performance festivals in the country are in New Mexico (the Santa Fe Opera Company) and in South Carolina (the Spoleto Festival). Each is in a lovely city with a certain reputation for old culture, on the tourist track. Each festival gets noticed because of its adventuresome coups. Santa Fe got to see the first production in America of the most important twentieth-century opera, Alban Berg's *Lulu*, incomplete in 1963 and complete in 1979. Charleston recently got to see the first performances of Arthur Miller's latest play, *The American Clock*. It doesn't seem to matter a whit that Charleston is in "the South" and that Santa Fe is not.

If any characteristic sets apart the way southern states patronize the arts it is the amount of help the arts get from state government—and again, the pattern holds almost as well for the states of the Southwest as it does for those of the Old Confederacy. In the major study of state arts funding done by the National Endowment for the Arts in 1974, seven of the eleven states with the lowest per capita government expenditures for the arts were states from the Old South.[8] The two lowest of the southern states were Florida and Texas, and interestingly enough their per capita rate was almost identical to California's. These figures have shifted somewhat in the intervening years, but I believe that the same principle holds today. There are important exceptions to the rule that southern states as states do not like to get involved in the arts—Virginia and North Carolina are the only two states with state-sponsored art museums—but the pattern is there.

---

8. *The State Arts Agencies in 1974: All Present, Accounted For* (Research Division Report #8, National Endowment for the Arts, April 1978), p. 62.

The relative indifference of state governments to the arts does not mean that the arts do not receive patronage in the Sunbelt states. There is even substantial governmental support from agencies on the national and local levels in the states with the least patronage. But at least some southern artistic institutions have turned with great success to the private sector for important contributions. Grant-making foundations have proliferated in the South as elsewhere, and these have proved to be of first importance in the survival of many artistic institutions. Corporations have been notably generous in providing support for the arts in southern cities. One rationale is that the presence of artistic attractions makes a city more desirable in hiring personnel. Houston has an impressive Combined Arts Corporate Campaign in which nearly two hundred corporations give amounts to be divided among the eight leading arts organizations. The most ambitious fundraising attempt by any southern arts organization is presently going on in Houston: the drive to fund the Wortham Theater, to house the opera and ballet, at a cost of $65 million. On a much smaller scale, a city like Memphis recently found it possible for its Arts Council to raise $288,550 out of a $600,000 budget from corporations and foundations, in support of local groups as well as to underwrite appearances of touring attractions.[9]

Many southern arts organizations are also encouraged by their boards to earn more substantial portions of their budgets than is the national norm. This is a matter of pride for some. Nina Vance, the late founder of the Alley Theatre, had to be approached by a foundation executive to receive the money to build her impressive physical plant in the late 1960s; she would not have gone to him. Over the years she could perhaps have been more adventuresome artistically if she had been willing to descend more often and more assiduously to fund raising, but she thought it wrong, or at least unseemly, to do so. In the South and Southwest it is often necessary to convince board members and donors that an artistic institution is as sensitive to sound business practices as to aesthetic matters.

Of course, plenty of southern artistic institutions have mastered all the

9. David A. Fryxell, "Winning by Cooperation," *Horizon*, 25, no. 4 (May/June 1982): 28–36.

rigors of learning to beg and to lobby. None of them is yet as lavishly endowed as the richest of the southern universities have become in recent
years—whether funded by the state, like the University of Texas; hand-
somely endowed, like Rice; or shored up by huge single gifts, like Emory
and Southern Methodist. But nearly all would like to be. The full flowering of the southern universities, in fact, may well go hand in hand with the
full flowering of the arts there. Universities are perhaps not the ideal pa-
trons and protectors of the arts, since they tend to breed a certain manda-
rinism impervious to the needs of a public. They have, however, provided
welcome havens for artists and smaller artistic institutions over the years—
not to speak of their role in training artists and educating audiences. As
more and more southern universities step up into the first rank of American schools, I think their sponsorship of the arts will grow in importance.
Already the University of North Carolina drama department, long a
pioneer in drama in the South, has spawned the Playmakers Repertory
Company. Important ties are also being established between existing arts
groups and universities, such as the Houston Grand Opera and the University of Houston. That relationship has enormously enriched the musical
life not only of the city of Houston and the state of Texas, but a whole
region of the country, through tours and workshops. The relatively new
Shepherd School of Music at Rice is also making a significant impact on
the Houston music world, and the Houston Symphony's new music director, Sergiu Comissiona, will be teaching part-time at the university. The
better and wealthier our universities get, the richer will be the results of
this mutual nourishment.

One must also point to the electronic media as potentially a great power
for equalization of the arts throughout the country. Some might fear that a
program such as "Live from Lincoln Center" might further centralize the
performing arts in New York and diminish the drawing power of local
companies. But I believe, and most observers agree, that a televised production of *Rigoletto* creates much larger audiences for local productions of
the opera. Certainly televised performances of the *Nutcracker* and video
versions of *A Christmas Carol* have not daunted the abundant proliferation
of these spectacles by smaller companies throughout the country. We will

certainly see a broadening selection of theater, music, opera, and dance productions from companies in the South and throughout the nation broadcast on television during the next few years. The Wolf Trap, Virginia, summer productions have been shown on a national Public Broadcasting System series, as have been a number of Spoleto productions from Charleston. The Houston Grand Opera and Dallas Civic Opera are among a handful of American companies to have all their productions heard in nationally syndicated radio series.

We may be able to look forward to the day when television has an effect on the arts much as it does today on sports, making possible elaborate productions that otherwise would have lost a great deal of money. Cable television, especially, holds this promise. If proceeds from such undertakings help to make artistic organizations in all parts of the country more equal to one another in quality and in wages offered, the institutions may find it necessary to emulate sports organizations in other ways. Symphonies and opera companies might have to set up a system to draft the best musicians coming out of the conservatories. Can you imagine the excitement of speculating whether the Atlanta Symphony will go with the double-bass player or the tympanist on its first-round pick?

Igor Stravinsky once noted that his oeuvre jutted off from the German mainstream of music at an angle, but also noted that in American slang an angle is an advantage. Will the late starts of the southern and southwestern cities enable them to learn from the experiences of the older American cities, and thus make their angle an advantage? It looks to me as though some cities are learning and some are not; much depends on who is making the decisions. A number of southern cities are still in the phase of building or remodeling halls, theaters, and museums, launched by the creation of Lincoln Center in the 1960s. Some have taken lessons from the experiences of New York and other cities with established arts activities to create more successful environments, and others have not seemed to profit from Yankee mistakes. We only learn from other peoples' experience when we are smart enough to figure out what that experience means.

To whatever extent artistic institutions in the South learn from each other and from similar institutions in other parts of the country, they will doubtlessly follow in the future, as they have in the past, the larger social trends that change the cities themselves. If the South continues to become more populous, more urban, and more like the rest of the country, arts institutions in the South will continue to become more prominent and less southern. Already most of the attempts to project a regional flavor in the arts result either in self-conscious kitsch (ceramic armadillos and cowboy boots) or in unconscious kitsch (the outdoor dramas of Paul Green that have proliferated in summertime evenings throughout the South). And the biggest cities will have the most visible and most internationalized arts institutions. If I have concentrated on activities in Houston and Dallas in this essay, it is not only because I know them best but because—since they are the biggest and richest cities in the region—the most noteworthy developments are taking place there.

And the desert shall rejoice and blossom abundantly, and rejoice even with joy and singing (and dancing and fiddling and acting and so forth). One may find it sad that homogenization between places and cultures seems to go along with modern improvements in the arts, as with so many other modern improvements. But when the Sahara sprouts oases and eventually turns into an Eden, perhaps we should not complain that one Edenic outpost looks pretty much the same as all the others.

☆ ☆ ☆ **6** ☆ ☆ ☆

The Southern City Today

NEAL R. PEIRCE

Significant urbanism is a latter-day phenomenon in the South. The traditional Southland's soul was always overwhelmingly rural. There were, to be sure, islands of exception from the earliest days—Charleston, Savannah, New Orleans, and a handful of others. But most of the South was a rough frontier in antebellum days, the dirt-poor white farmers outnumbering the plantation gentility that would later be enshrined in the region's lore. "Town" was a tiny county seat, not a major metropolis. And during the decades of the latter nineteenth and early twentieth centuries, when the North was embarked on its historic era of industrialization and urbanization, the South retained its overwhelmingly rural flavor. There were, of course, exceptions: here and there a gritty industrial city like Birmingham and the textile towns of the Piedmont. But until World War II the vast majority of the South's people lived on farms or in little villages. In Mississippi, the most rural of all, the figure was 83 percent.

One might wish that as the South began to urbanize in an earnest way in the mid-twentieth century, it had followed the pattern of its early cities. It might have looked to Savannah, where founder James Oglethorpe devised one of the most ingenious and pleasing to the human spirit of all American town plans—a series of modular units, called "wards," each with public buildings and some forty residential lots and a public square at the center, laid out one neatly beside the other, the public squares creating a unique sense of intimacy and neighborhood. Or to Charleston, with its rich his-

tory as the first South Carolina settlement in 1670, its golden era of trade
and leisured planter aristocracy in colonial days, its leadership in the
American Revolution, its preeminent role in nullification and finally secession—a city in which many people of Dixie have long believed the Holy
Grail of their southernhood to be somehow enshrined. Or even to New
Orleans, with its rich gumbo-mélange of French and Spanish and Af-
rican and Latin and Irish and German and Italian and English ancestry, its
port window to the continental hinterland upstream and the world out to
sea. Today, of course, there is still a Savannah, forever a treasure among
American cities, happily spared the economic "progress" that engulfed and
destroyed any of the old Atlanta overlooked by Sherman. Charleston continues, its hubris well intact, its historic preservation flourishing if one can
see past the mountains of military establishment ensnared for it by the
likes of L. Mendel Rivers. New Orleans retains its hedonism and gastronomic delicacy, its leafy Garden District, its essential bawdiness with a
surfeit of tourist overlay.

But today one thinks of southern city, and what springs first to mind?
Those great concrete and glass monoliths—the "new" Atlanta where the
airways and bankers meet, Houston with its mushroom-like growth of our
energy era, the "Big D" of the Dallas-Fort Worth combine. Cities of
unique character: Memphis by the Delta, Nashville of country music fame,
St. Petersburg for twilight years, San Antonio for the military and sheer
urban delight along the Paseo del Rio. And now, perhaps most fascinating
of all, Miami—the oldest tourist town turned into the de facto trade and
banking capital of South America, its rapidly expanding Cuban population
an ethnic confirmation of the economic change. But primarily the southern city of today is neither massive nor characterful. It is a place like the
prospering Piedmont cities of Charlotte, Greenville, Columbia, or Greensboro. If you compare the population sizes of southern cities with others
across the nation, you find many more than average in the 50,000-to-
200,000 population range, and then, at the top of the scale, only a third of
the national average of those of one million or more. Smaller metropolitan
areas and cities, few of the largest metropolises—this is the urban South
today. And in a sense, that may be a very real asset. For it is in smaller and

medium-sized cities that many planners, as well as polls of residents, indicate a greater potential for "livability." Such cities can also provide a cross-
section of necessary urban services without the disadvantages (including
significantly higher service costs and taxes) that seem to afflict the nation's
largest cities. They are more manageable; they have a much thinner overlay
of proliferating and competing governmental units than their larger northern counterparts.

Beyond such generalities, it becomes exceedingly difficult to generalize
about the southern city of our time. Marshall Kaplan, in a study prepared
for the White House at the beginning of Jimmy Carter's administration,[1]
noted that "cities of the South and Southwest are viewed en masse as
growing dynamic centers with growing employment bases, upward pressures on income, adequate infrastructure and fiscal surpluses." Yet when
one pokes below the surface, Kaplan observed, this is not a universal
truth—the same conclusion reached by economists preparing a 1980 set of
papers on the southern city today for the Southern Growth Policies Board.
Rather, Kaplan suggested, "if the cities of the South can be characterized
in any way, it is by diversity. Not all of them are growing. And, a significant number are experiencing both population and economic decline,
downward trends in per capita income levels, shrinking tax bases and the
fiscal 'squeeze' associated with such conditions—a profile strikingly similar
to that of the older industrial centers of the Northeast." This does not
mean that many if any southern cities stand at the kind of fiscal precipice
faced by mid-Atlantic or midwestern cities that are presently seeing their
heavy industry melt away, a trend that has created severe repercussions for
those northern cities. The generally healthy, growth-oriented economic
setting of the South provides a far more hospitable setting for its cities.

Yet just because a southern city, on the average, reflects a low unemployment rate and lacks the severest indicators of fiscal and economic distress,
we cannot assume that there are not "pockets of poverty" in which conditions may be every bit as adverse as some of the most hard-hit northern

---

1. *Growth and the Cities of the South: A Study in Diversity* (Washington, D. C.: White House
Conference on Balanced Growth and Economic Development, 1977).

cities. And, suggests Kaplan, "The fact that a metropolitan area as a whole is experiencing dynamic growth does not signify its central city is sharing equally in that growth. In fact, quite significant and increasing suburban/ center city disparities exist in some Southern areas which are adversely affecting economic growth, service needs, revenue sources and the fiscal health of the center city." The lesson seems clear enough: such cities, hemmed in by ancient borders, can suffer in the midst of a sea of affluence.

The broad-scale annexation on which a number of southern cities have embarked can and does relieve the overall tax burden; to the degree that social and urban decay problems are addressed, the entire area, including its wealthy suburban hinterland, shoulders a share of the burden. It is no accident that such cities as Houston, Nashville, and Jacksonville, able to expand their borders rapidly through annexation or metropolitan-wide government, tend to be in healthier fiscal shape than "ringed in" cities such as Atlanta, Richmond, New Orleans, and Louisville. Indeed, the South has had more success than virtually any other region of the United States in effecting city-county consolidations—even though, as fiscal disparities have increased between the center cities and their hinterlands, the obstacles to such mergers have risen rapidly, so that we may see few if any more in the near future. Lower municipal wages, less public worker unionization, and lower expectations of a high level of city services are all factors that make southern cities places in which the weight of taxation is far lower than in most of the North. In addition, the state share of the state-local financing responsibility is generally greater in the South than in the North, and there is greater reliance on sales and payroll taxes than the typically inelastic property taxes that the Northeast and Midwest rely upon so heavily. But the ancient discriminatory practice of many white southern establishments—providing adequate services, including paved streets, high-quality street lighting, sewers, and other facilities for the "better" parts of town, while black and poor white neighborhoods must subsist with unpaved streets and open sewers—has not altogether vanished. And in many of the booming Sunbelt metropolises, engaged in a helter-skelter rush for growth at any price, essential public infrastructure is not built, or is shabbily built. Later, the piper must be paid, a hard fact that more and more southern cities will be facing in the coming years.

Migration is yet another crucial variable in the urban Southland today. One migratory stream is that of skilled workers and an "executive" class that has been a massive economic advantage for such cities as Houston, Dallas, Charlotte, Orlando, and Columbia. A second group is largely rural, black folk migrating into the cities. Census estimates for the 1970–1975 period showed that 61 percent of all rural blacks who moved into cities around the United States moved into cities of the South. And since the South still held, in the 1970s, more than 50 percent of the nation's blacks, and rural black birth rates were exceptionally high compared to other population groups, the prospect for increasingly black (and poor) southern cities remains very real. In 1977 the *New York Times* quoted Lamond Godwin, former southeastern director of the National Rural Center, as saying, "Rural black families are producing enough children to populate the urban areas and still maintain a constant rural population. The South is following the lead of the North in using the city as an economic dumping ground." And all of this, Mr. Godwin said, "could very well throw a monkey wrench into the dreams of the Sunbelt."[2] By 1980 Atlanta's population was 66.6 percent black, New Orleans's 55.3 percent, Birmingham's 55.6 percent, Shreveport's 41.1 percent, Jackson's 47.0 percent, and Richmond's 51.3 percent. Some of the most despair-ridden black slums in America are to be found in these cities, along with some of the cruelest patterns of suburban discrimination against the inner city, exemplified by the callous attitudes of Jefferson and Plaquemines parishes toward New Orleans, or of Henrico and Chesterfield counties toward Richmond.

The encouraging side of black development in southern cities has been that blacks have grown in political power: in the late 1970s, for instance, Ernest ("Dutch") Morial was elected mayor of New Orleans, and Maynard Jackson and then Andrew Young became mayors of Atlanta. Of all the changes, the most dramatic seemed to be in Birmingham, a town that progressed from the days of "Bull" Connor and his police dogs to the 1979 election of Richard Arrington, a highly regarded black mayor. In sheer numbers, however, it has been small southern cities—below 50,000 in

2. Wayne King, "Blacks Are Now Discovering Urban Ills in Southern Cities," *New York Times*, May 8, 1977.

population—that have elected black mayors or black majorities to their city councils.

Another great urban migration of minorities who sometimes become majorities is that of Hispanics—Cubans in the Miami area, Mexican-Americans in all of the great Texas cities. San Antonio, El Paso, and Brownsville are heavily Hispanic in complexion, with growing political power to match. Houston, Dallas, and other major Texas cities all have growing Hispanic minorities. There are poverty-ridden barrios in such cities, yet as the Cubans have illustrated in Florida, and Mexican-Americans in many areas of Texas cities, there is an upward economic mobility that bodes well for the future.

A final major migration trend of the urban South has been of white, middle-class native southern folk to the suburbs of the region. All of this poses varied problems for the South's center cities: their prospects of realizing net income gains and capturing a larger tax base are dependent on the degree to which they can attract northern emigrés, hold back suburbanization of their middle classes, and restrict in-migration of poor blacks and Hispanics. To the extent that the suburbs capture the lion's share of more affluent immigrants, the most perplexing problem is the present economic base and future economic prospect of the city proper.

Blacks and Hispanics sometimes compete, in some locations bitterly, for jobs and economic opportunity—a situation most dramatic in Miami, where black resentment against a perceived preference for Cubans was said to be one of the factors that triggered the Liberty City riots of 1980, among the most brutal racial conflicts in United States history. Yet in gaining political power, the two groups have shared an interest: to see cities divided into individual councilmanic districts, so that they have a greater opportunity to gain council seats and thus significant political influence. A major watershed, for instance, was the 1975 extension of the Voting Rights Act to permit the U.S. Department of Justice to review electoral districts and annexations in states such as Texas.[3] In crucial 1979 elections, Houston's

3. The future application of the Voting Rights Act in city representation cases was thrown into doubt by the April 22, 1980, decision of the United States Supreme Court, on a six-to-three vote, reversing lower court decisions that had ruled the at-large election of city commis-

council, previously elected all at-large, suddenly had geographical districts for nine of its fourteen seats and saw the election of three blacks, the first Mexican-American council member, and two women. Dallas's new council included a Chicano who was previously a leader of the fiery "Brown Berets" organization, along with two blacks and some white members who were clearly at odds with the downtown business interests that have so long dominated Dallas. In a city like Houston, such elections can make a critical difference. Many of the poor, Hispanic areas of the inner city, for example, are without curbs or gutters. Flooding, sewer backups, and pot-holed streets are constant problems. Land subsidence and lack of trash disposal sites confound city hall. Houston's city government (in stark contrast to Dallas's) has long been a model of nonprofessional management. "Sweetheart" political relationships that permit a burgeoning of down-town office towers while the neighborhoods decline are likely to come un-der effective political attack in a more "democratic" era. The new Houston mayor, Kathy Whitmire, is aggressively addressing the issues of too-rapid and unplanned growth, and is bringing effective management techniques to a city that hitherto has been run inefficiently. The developers do not "own" her, and her strongest support comes from the new business and professional elites for whom "quality of life" is the urban issue. And in San Antonio, Henry Cisneros, the first Mexican-American mayor of a major United States city, has brought to city hall significant professionalism and ingenuity in planning a high technology future for his city's people.

When the history of the southern city in the twentieth century is writ-ten, the coincidence of Dixie urbanism and the era of unfettered auto-mobility will doubtless loom large. With a few exceptions—the rapid rail systems of Atlanta and Miami, or the remnants of New Orleans's grand old trolley car system—the growth pattern has been one of careless, incessant sprawl and the lack of a decent mass transportation system. A typical pic-

---

sioners in Mobile, Alabama, as unconstitutionally diluting the voting strength of blacks—who comprise about thirty-five percent of Mobile's population but never have elected one of their own to the three-member commission. The Court said plaintiffs must prove that at-large systems have been adopted or maintained for the purpose of discriminating against mi-nority voters.

ture was painted by urban reporter Mitch Mendelson in the September 29, 1980, edition of the *Birmingham Post-Herald:*

> The 22-year-old bus lurches and heaves over the hills of Crestwood. On one particularly steep climb, you wonder if the bus, which looks older than its driver, will make it.
>
> If it is hot this afternoon or tomorrow—as it was last week—you and your fellow riders will be sweat-soaked as you look out at passing cars, each with one passenger, each with its windows closed to keep out the heat and keep in the air conditioning.
>
> Today, for the dubious privilege of riding this noisy, swaying bus, which may not get you home, which stops running at 5:30 P.M., which doesn't run on Saturday, you paid 80 cents. You and your 30,000 fellow riders of the Birmingham-Jefferson County Transit Authority have the curious distinction of paying the highest public transit fare in the country.

On the average, fewer than 5 percent of southern commuters in 1980 were using public transportation, and the image of the systems was often "okay for somebody else"—often meaning the black or poor. There were some signs of improvement on the transit front—the aggressive promotion of the Hop-A-Bus shuttle in downtown Dallas, more park-and-ride lots outside of city centers, Houston's proposed $2.1 billion rail and subway transit system and $16 billion Regional Mobility Plan, breakthroughs in carpooling and vanpooling in which Knoxville (principally because of the Tennessee Valley Authority's leadership) was considered to be one of the most advanced cities in the United States. But until the South is hit by even more expensive gasoline, or actual gasoline shortages, the political constituency for an adequate mass transit system appears to be lacking.

The automobile has contributed to another phenomenon: tasteless sprawl development. Even some southern city "centers" became embodiments of the repulsive twentieth century invention of gasoline- and hamburger-alleys, loaded with plastic signs and billboards, gasoline stations, convenience marts, and the like. An example: the "instant" city of Arlington, Texas, close to the Dallas-Fort Worth Regional Airport, which ballooned in population yet developed no discernible city center whatever and was considered by some the fast-food capital of the United States. The roads leading into and out of virtually every southern city replicated that theme. The same phenomenon, of course, afflicted many of the nation's other regions, but the South's status as a region of fast-growing, auto-mobile-age cities seemed to make the situation even worse than elsewhere. The indifference with which southerners watched suburban shopping malls siphon off retailing and the vitality of the older city and town centers was a case in point. In July 1979 *South* magazine surveyed the scene in a virtual paean of praise for the malls and disregard of the city centers. "The Passing of Downtown Shopping," read the headline, with this subhead: "Saving Southern downtowns as retail shopping centers, explain experts, may be like trying to save snowballs in July. Women shoppers want se-curity, convenience—open space parking close to a mall." The survey found that virtually every major national or regionally-based retail store chain—Sears, J. C. Penney, Montgomery Ward, J. B. Ivey & Co., Belk's, Dillard's, Maas Bros., Cain-Sloan—was planning to expand in suburban malls, not downtown, where they were found to be closing old, outmoded stores. Said a Sears executive in Atlanta: "You won't find us opening any stores downtown, no matter how much facelifting they do." The survey reported that twenty-three southern cities had tried to equal the suburban shopping centers by opening their own downtown malls between 1972 and 1979, but that only six—Anniston, Huntsville, Jacksonville, Nashville, Norfolk, and Tampa—reported an increase in retail sales after the down-town malls opened their doors.

Nonstop sprawl development, retail abandonments of downtowns, the lack of mass transit, the South's aversion to tough zoning or state or local land-use planning controls: do all these presage an eventual demise of the southern city as a place of principal human activity, indeed a demise before the southern city has even had an age in which to flower? The answer may be yes. But by 1980 there were reports from across the region of efforts to stem the tide, efforts that conceivably would bear fruit during the last two decades of the century. Many cities were, for instance, engaged in intensive downtown redevelopment efforts—among them Savannah, Dallas, Jacksonville, Norfolk, Charlottesville, Nashville, New Orleans, Little Rock, Greenville, Atlanta, Louisville, Tulsa, Oklahoma City, Birmingham, and Charleston, West Virginia. Charleston, with some strategic aid from the Carter White House, fought off the efforts of developers to build a massive retailing complex outside of the city and thus was able to move ahead with its impressive downtown retailing and capitol mall project.

A central problem has been the quality—one might say the true urbanity—of many of the new South's downtown efforts. Philip Morris described the situation well in the January 1980 issue of *Southern Living:* "The worst that has happened to most downtowns is the random demolition of buildings for ground-level parking lots, depriving the core of its architectural wealth, its physical tightness, its sense of place. There is nothing more depressing than seeing a shiny new thirty-story office tower with blocks all around wiped out to serve parking needs."[4] Indeed, my own observation is that the South suffers from parking lot devastation more than any other region of the nation. That, along with a lack of a mix of people-drawing, mutually supportive business, entertainment, and commercial activities in the South's inner cities, has often created an atmosphere that Morris describes as "pitifully sub-urban."

Perhaps the greatest disappointment of all has been the Cinderella city of the postwar South: Atlanta. During the 1960s and 1970s one towering "megastructure" after another rose along Peachtree Street or in its immediate environs. The Atlanta downtown, which the *Saturday Evening Post* had described in 1945 as "less attractive than Birmingham's," became a magnet for businessmen and conventioneers from across the continent, the city itself serving as the regional headquarters of dozens of major corporations and government departments (not to mention its own state capitol and firms such as Coca-Cola). At the end of the 1960s John Portman's Hyatt Regency Hotel and connected Peachtree Center became a wonder for travelers; in the seventies came even more impressive megastructures, including the world's tallest hotel. Yet using Atlanta as my prime example, I felt compelled to ask in a 1977 newspaper column: "Must the architectural

---

4. Philip Morris, "Shaping Livable Southern Cities," *Southern Living*, January 1980.

behemoths, cold and forbidding exercises in the egotism of architects and the boosterism of big business, invariably generate 'bombed out' belts of parking lots, freeway ramps, 'porno' shops and high-crime zones around their peripheries?" The scene around the Peachtree Street megastructures, I noted, was one of urban devastation, from empty lots to ugly old warehouses. Visiting conventioneers would hesitate to step outside of the enclosed, high-security environment of their hotel complexes at night. The city had few of the small and colorful shops, restaurants, galleries, walking spaces, and gathering places for people that give a city character. The Atlanta experience, it seemed to me, indicated that a downtown business establishment left to its own devices will opt for monumentalism and ignore the essential human element of city-building. And the price paid was more than lack of inner-city livability. Between 1955 and 1965 alone, 15 percent of Atlanta's people were displaced by urban renewal and highways that plowed through established neighborhoods.

By the mid-1970s a vigorous neighborhood movement had formed in Atlanta, first to fight freeways, then to expand into the political arena and help to elect one of its antifreeway allies, Maynard Jackson, as Atlanta's first black mayor. Intent on new freeways and jealous of its power, the Atlanta business establishment, the little group that had once made the essential decisions over lunch at the Commerce Club, at first viewed Jackson and the neighborhoods as dangerous enemies. But power recognizes power; with Central Atlanta Progress taking the lead for business, confrontation was yielding to accommodation. As CAP president Dan Sweat said: "We began to see the neighborhoods are the first line of defense for the economy of downtown, that central Atlanta can't afford to be surrounded by a ring of slums." To fight redlining of poor neighborhoods, CAP worked with neighborhood groups and the banks to set up a $62.5 million mortgage consortium for borderline risks. And CAP began to focus on such areas as the thirty-six-block Fairlie-Poplar area that flanks Peachtree Street from Five Points, the old retail-business heart of the city, to Peachtree Center. The hope was that the area, as Sweat put it, might become "a high-grade So-Ho" with art galleries, antique stores, restaurants, and a latter-day wave of market-rate inner-city housing. To say that all suddenly became sweetness and light in Atlanta would be a gross error. More mega-structures were still on the drawing boards; the expectation of their com-ing inflated inner-city land values to disparage low-rise, more characterful development. Some freeway battles continued, even with the first leg of the MARTA subway system in operation. And the immense, indeed fearful income disparities between white and black Atlantans continued, together with many race-related crimes. Yet Atlanta's governing "system," by 1980, was more open. And to some degree the same process—a questioning of unrestrained megastructure building, a growth of neighborhood power, an interest in pedestrian-oriented areas—was under way in many cities across the Southland.

Physically, the evidence was becoming apparent. One saw it in Savan-nah's historic district, including its twelve-block stretch of nineteenth-century cotton warehouses converted into restaurants, stores, museums, and a small but handsome waterfront park. In Louisville's $87 million Ken-tucky Cultural Complex on the banks of the Ohio River, a landmark mixed-use development including theaters, an art school and gallery, offices, apart-ments, shops, and parkland. In the ambitious, multiuse, pedestrian-oriented Arkansas River development in Tulsa. In Nashville's plans for a downtown apartment district to be centered on a park facing the restored home of the Grand Ole Opry (an area robbed of its one-time vibrance by the Opry's 1970s flight to a new suburbanized amusement-park setting). The Nashville apartments, in fact, suggested that residentially-oriented inner-city mixed use development was finally coming of age in the South, its slow beginnings notwithstanding.[5] One found the trend in Atlanta's Mid-town, between downtown and Colony Square, where individual house renovation was flourishing along tree-lined streets and net residential de-velopment was being fitted carefully into the traditional pattern. It was ap-parent, too, in Natchez, Mississippi, where new life was being injected into downtown through the renovation of the upper floors of old commer-cial buildings. Inner-city residential development was rising in Memphis,

5. For further background, see Philip Morris, "When People Live Close," *Southern Living*, November 1980.

particularly in the Cotton Row Historic District. In Austin, Texas, developers built an imaginative cluster of thirty-four new owner-occupied buildings on two acres of sloping, tree-studded land close to its downtown core. Charlotte's Fourth Ward, a stone's throw from the city's handsome new arts center, Spirit Square, had won a fresh lease on life with the restoration of old houses and also infill development of a handsome group of brick townhouses known as Hackberry Place. Also in the North Carolina Piedmont, Winston-Salem was building on its distinguished fine arts background (the city is home of the world-famed North Carolina School of the Arts) to build an impressive multipurpose arts complex as the keystone of its belated inner-city development effort. The $1-billion-plus Houston Center project—with office towers, hotels, six thousand anticipated condominiums, and a sixteen-story shopping arcade running for two elevated blocks beneath a glass canopy—will create a downtown version of suburban Houston's spectacularly successful Galleria mixed-use development. Yet as promising as all these developments were, the traveler through the Southland's cities in the early 1980s had to conclude that true urbanism was still more promise than reality. The last two decades of the century will decide whether the year 2000 will bring a rich, variegated urban South, valuing historic preservation as much as the cold commercialism of single-purpose "central business districts," the arts and street life as much as parking lots—or rather, tiny outposts of urbanity in a sea of sprawl engulfing the region's once-lovely woodland, coastal, and hill regions.

One of the most dramatic decisions to come, for instance, centers on Columbia's huge 550-acre "Main Street West" area stretching from the State Capitol and downtown business district to the banks of the Congaree River. Today that area is largely vacant: it has a state prison, the governor's mansion, a sprinkling of warehouses, and a few hundred houses of low-income residents, almost all black. It is an area that calls out for comprehensive, integrated planning. Unguided, one can easily imagine the future: a little forest of Dairy Queens, Burger Kings, Pizza Huts, perhaps a Holiday or Ramada Inn. Garish signs. Dull and faceless apartment houses—if any. Monolithic state government buildings. Acres of parking lots. A place without tone, connection, or integrity—coupled most likely with eviction of the last remnants of the black community. Alternatively, Main Street West might be developed to capitalize on a prize location. The city might push to complete the large river-front park project now in the planning stage, including every attraction from hiking and biking trails to observation decks, historic sites and boat trips, a South Carolina Performing Arts Center and Twentieth Century Fox news film library, and the charm of a nineteenth-century canal that parallels the river. Then, between the river and canal and the city center, Columbia could build a set of greenways providing pedestrian and bicycle links. The plan should include not only varieties of offices and shops, but ideally quantities of medium-density housing (town houses, garden apartments, and the like) to draw the young professionals working for the state government, the University of South Carolina, or in the downtown business district. In fact, all these ideas were being discussed in Columbia—including ways to preserve housing for the low-income residents of the area. Whether or not the plans come to fruition will depend on Columbia's civic and political leaders—their foresight and tenacity, their willingness to enter into creative partnerships between the public and private sectors, and their social vision.

In discussions of all things southern, the question of race is never far below the surface. And so one does well to end with a question: can the southern city be a creative force for alleviating this age-old pain of the region? A rapid migration of poor rural blacks into the city's regions will certainly not make that task easy, any more than it has in the North; nor will the inequities in the criminal justice system that led, even in 1980, to racial outbreaks in such cities as Miami and Chattanooga. The ultimate responsibility in the criminal justice area should lie not with cities alone, but also with the states. One of the most discouraging phenomena is to see appeals to the federal government for intervention after a Miami-style outbreak, when it is the ongoing responsibility of the state government to guarantee professional police protection and a fair, balanced court system in all the counties and municipalities. The successful biracial urban society, in the South as well as elsewhere in America, will require increasing and close cooperation between government and the private sector to draw minorities into the economic mainstream, to give them a stake in the system. Such an approach will have to begin with close curriculum cooperation between the schools and private business. Then it should proceed to such efforts as one-on-one consultation between successful white-led businesses and striving black or Hispanic enterprises. Such cooperation is almost totally lacking today, a disturbing portent for the future.

In the housing area, one may be marginally more optimistic—not that most poor minorities in southern cities do not continue to live in dreadfully inadequate housing. In New Orleans, for instance, one can find some of the most wretched and dangerous public housing projects in the country. Private housing for the poor is often just as bad; the shotgun-house slum has not yet passed into history, for instance, and San Antonio's poor, brawling barrios must be seen to be believed. Yet compared to the North, public housing in most southern cities generally offers a degree of physical maintenance, civic orderliness, sometimes even pleasing environment, rarely found in other parts of the nation. Perhaps it is because southern blacks, for all the injustices they have suffered, feel more an indigenous part of the community than their brethren in transplanted situations in the North. If southern cities can nurture those feelings of identity and mutual interest, then minority housing conditions in the region might be saved the jungle-like perils of many northern ghettoes.

A showcase of what could be achieved across the South is found in Savannah, where half of the twelve hundred structures in the architecturally distinguished old Victorian District are being rehabilitated for and rented back to their poor black tenants. The original impetus for this effort came from investment banker Leopold Adler II, descendant of an old Savannah family and former president of the Historic Savannah Foundation (the group that earlier sparked the preservation and restoration of eight hundred buildings in the heart of the historic district laid out by Oglethorpe so many centuries ago). Now under Savannah Landmark's biracial board, multiple federal housing subsidy programs have been tapped to create the financing for the high-quality restoration of Victorian District homes for the poor. The rest of the housing restoration—houses for middle- and upper-income people, mostly white, but also some black—is being done privately. The result could be one of the most racially and economically diverse neighborhoods in America. It is the initiative, the sensitivity of groups such as Savannah Landmark, that give one some hope for the southern city in our time.

7

☆ ☆ ☆ ☆ ☆ ☆

Dixiefied National Politics
Sameness with a Difference

BRANDT AYERS

There is a blood-secret to southern politics, an ache so old that it has almost become a friend, a point of reference that defines "us" as opposed to "them." It is this deeper mystery of the southern soul—the self-respect issue—that makes the heart of Dixie so hard to understand for political analysts from outside the region. Prying, pick-lock pollsters and reporters sifting through the litter left by the 1982 elections could draw some outrageously wrong conclusions unless they looked beneath the surface. To wit:

False Prophecy No. 1. The emergence of a two-party South has been dealt a severely retarding blow by heavy Republican losses in the region, including a net loss of four seats in the House of Representatives and a net gain of twelve Democratic seats.

False Prophecy No. 2. Southern politics is so gothic, so utterly irrational, that it defies understanding. Because the region has so little in common with the rest of the country, no presidential candidate from the South stands a chance—especially considering Jimmy Carter of sour memory.

False Prophecy No. 3. Proof of the South's mysterious political behavior can be found in the black-white coalition that swept George Wallace back into the Alabama statehouse. That means the populists' old, forlorn hope for a black-white economic alliance has finally come true. George Wallace is truly the answer to Martin Luther King's dream.

How are presidential candidates from outside the region ever to comprehend the heart of Dixie, that enigma wrapped in an artichoke? It is a simple three-stage process: understand the spiritual issues, the cultural mysteries of the region; then absorb the mechanical, policy issues; and finally, devise language that gets in touch with both simultaneously. This has proved to be somewhat difficult, even for many politicians and journalists who are natives. Where do we begin?

First, let's dispose of the dream of Dr. King and the populists. George Wallace isn't exactly what Dr. King had in mind. Wallace's black-white coalition is stuck together with water and flour. Against his Republican challenger, Montgomery mayor Emory Folmar, Wallace got 91 percent of the vote in a representative black box in my home town, Carver Community Center. But in the Democratic runoff against the state's progressive young lieutenant governor, George McMillan, Wallace got less than 16 percent in the same box. Folmar himself was the difference. Had he been a GOP candidate in the mold of Governor Lamar Alexander of Tennessee or Governor David Treen of Louisiana, he might have won. But he wasn't. Folmar is a man of muscular self-confidence who enjoys his macho image. As mayor he carried a gun, went on police raids, and talked with fiercely delicious pleasure about punishing transgressors. Folmar unwittingly reminded blacks of the old southern cop who didn't bother with the legal technicality of a search warrant before entering a black man's home. Of course, a less-than-best Republican nominee wasn't the sole deciding factor in the race. Alabama and Michigan had been competing through the year for the distinction of having the nation's highest unemployment rate. Many working-class whites and blacks who had been hurt or frightened by the recession remembered that they had been better off when Wallace was governor. Wallace also made it easier for blacks to support him because of his public admission that he was wrong about segregation.

The death of racial politics is just one of a cluster of changes that has transformed a region that was once characterized solely by poverty, pellagra, and prejudice. Conversation with southern governors is—given the differences between, say, Mississippi and Virginia—conversation about the national agenda: urban problems, crime, adjusting economically and educationally to a post-industrial economy. The policy agenda of the urban-industrial South isn't much different from that of California or New York. But underneath our store-bought Saks Fifth Avenue suits and, most especially, underneath our working-class coveralls, we conceal a symbol of distinctiveness with lasting power. It is a vestigial tail called history. The Yale historian C. Vann Woodward, who has taught generations of southerners why their families are different, explains the region's distinctiveness as the result of thoroughly un-American experiences: defeat in war, persistent poverty, and stubborn defense of the morally indefensible, which leads to conscious or unconscious guilt.

In the South's long trek down through history it has sought something even more important than material comfort; it has sought self-respect. The journey has been hard, because along the way the South has been scorned for its poverty, its backward country ways, and for the long moral lapse of slavery and then segregation. Scorn is a terrible weapon, because it does not aim for a victory of arms and ideals. Instead, it seeks the final defeat: destruction of the human spirit. George Wallace knows that. He knows that a scorned people need stereotypes to defend their own sense of self-worth. He has made a career of championing the little man and kicking the arrogant or pompous in the seat of the pants.

As a third-party candidate in 1968 Wallace spoke out for "the good little people who need representation as much as the elite folks who run the major parties in this country and look down their noses at you and me." There was a good deal of talk about scorn, that old psychological ache, during the presidential primaries of 1976. At the courthouse cafe, the courthouse barbershop, and other universities of common wisdom in my home town, a typical conversation would include the following: "If 'they' take the nomination away from Carter, 'they'll' never let us live it down. It'll be another hundred years before any southerner has a chance." But the emotional wallop of the self-respect issue was unleashed by George Wallace during the Democratic runoff election in 1982 with an intensity that surprised even long-time students of southern politics. The CBS reporter Mike Wallace was hauled around as a punching bag of pomposity for the George Wallace campaign. The former governor told crowds that the television reporter criticized overcrowding in Alabama prisons during an interview. George Wallace answered, "You folks at CBS are so brilliant and so powerful. Why don't you go to the cemetery and raise those people they killed from the dead and ask *them* what they think of the space *they* got—down there [in the grave]?" Crowds howled. Through Wallace they themselves were out-witting that cocky, fast-talking, big-shot reporter. A man who won report-ers' respect as one of the all-time most able White House press secretaries, Jody Powell, chuckled but wasn't surprised at the reaction that Wallace's counter-punch received. "One of the reasons you can still get folks to stand up and cheer by taking a poke at arrogance looking down its nose at com-mon folks is because people are still doing it," said Powell. "It shouldn't surprise the people doing it when they get their noses rearranged—whether they're looking down on rural whites or city blacks."[1]

Another man, witness to much of the worst of southern politics and a creative leader in some of its best moments, also testifies that the self-respect issue still has force. "It surely *is* still there," says Governor William Winter of Mississippi. He advises presidential candidates of both parties: "Don't ignore us, don't take us for granted, and for goodness sake, don't put us down. This is not said with the old, bitter inferiority complex of the past. The old injustices have given way to new habits of political and social life; we have no apologies to make to anyone. We're going to insist on participating on a fair and totally equal basis in the decisionmaking process and in the benefits that come from being part of this country."

What does all this mean to presidential candidates who want to harvest the South's rich electoral vote that was increased by eight in the last cen-sus? Will the South succumb to a demagogic appeal to the touchy, defen-sive pride of rural and working-class whites who are quick to sniff the slightest whiff of condescension? Hardly. There are better ways, but more of that later. One of the things that makes southern politics so tricky is that its distinctiveness is marbled through a surface mass of issues that are simi-lar to the issues debated in the rest of the country. The South represents sameness—with a difference. For instance, the day is long past when a Re-

---

1. All quotations are derived from telephone interviews by the author.

publican candidate's getting two votes is prima facie evidence of vote fraud. The two-party South is here to stay—despite some reversals in the general elections of 1982. The solid South was broken like a pyramid of billiard balls in 1952 when Dwight David Eisenhower carried Florida, Tennessee, Texas, and Virginia. Only in 1976 did the strong affinity of the South for a credible candidate of its own reassemble an almost solid South behind Georgian Jimmy Carter. That was temporary. While Republicans held only two governorships after the 1982 elections, they were in good shape in the United States Senate; only Arkansas and Louisiana had two Democratic senators. Governor Charles R. ("Chuck") Robb, who recovered the Virginia statehouse for the Democrats in 1981, could have been speaking for all the region's Democratic governors when he said, "I don't think the political loyalties of the older generation will show anything like as much among the younger generation." Mississippi governor Winter certainly agreed: "As long as Republicans run good candidates, they're going to win most of the races; no Democrat without credentials will automatically get elected."

Bill Winter has had some experience with good Republican candidates in his state: U.S. Senator Thad Cochran and U.S. Representative Trent Lott. They are among the region's moderate Republican leadership with a firm grip on their seats. That wing of the party is best typified by the much-admired Senate majority leader Howard Baker of Tennessee and a former aide, Governor Lamar Alexander. "I think that moderate leadership is what the rank and file of the South is looking for," says Winter. But there is another tribal leader competing for the soul of the GOP in Dixie. Will southern Republicans follow Senator Jesse Helms of North Carolina on his nostalgic return to Waltons' Mountain? Senator Helms reads the cultural mysteries and values of his native region almost as well as George Wallace. He understands instinctively the popular appeal of the long-running television series; he represents the 1930s past, not so much as it was in reality, but through the romantic filter of memory. Those were the days of God-centered family virtues. Grandpa and Grandma weren't sent to a nursing home; they lived right there with the family, sharing their love and wisdom with the grandchildren. The family shared the chores and the worship, and if they had to, did without, uncomplaining. The whole family listened to the simple words of Franklin Roosevelt on the radio, words that soothed their fears and gave them hope. Presidents were respected back then, and so was the authority of teachers and parents. Children who misbehaved at school would expect a good hiding with a hickory switch at home—and got it, but with love. That era was ordered, disciplined, loving, understandable, and thus comfortably safe. The social issues that are rooted in those memories and that generated the "Moral Majority" and its high priests, like Senator Helms, need not be sneered at. Moderate politicians cannot lead people whose feelings they misunderstand. Southerners found it hard to comprehend the chaotic classrooms and unruly college students of the 1960s and 1970s. Education to them has always been priceless—the only way out of poverty and scorn. The natural patriotism of the average southerner was offended by protests against the Vietnam war, and America's loss in Indochina was a fresh weal on top of an old bruise, a second Lost Cause.

Jesse Helms understood. He saw that southerners were hurt and confused. He fashioned an emotional appeal to those old values, and North Carolinians responded—for a time. His legislative program was built around those old, moral verities. He and his colleague, Senator John East, even promised to solve the mystery of creation—the question of when life begins—by a majority vote of 535 politicians in Congress. But that program did not seem relevant in 1982 to people who were alarmed by an uncertain economic future. North Carolina's brilliant Democratic governor, Jim Hunt, offered people a clear path to better jobs in a more secure economic future. North Carolinians rejected all six candidates for the U.S. House of Representatives backed by Helms and turned out two Republican congressmen, replacing them with Democrats. In two years, Governor Hunt is likely to send Senator Helms home alone to Waltons' Mountain.

Moderate Republican leaders don't snicker at the powerful feelings tapped by the Helms forces, but they are impatient with emotional detours when the entire international economic system is going through a turbulent revolution. They think that Helms represents the wave of the past and that the future belongs to political leaders who try to understand the present realities and who try to give their people the pride and confidence to face the future. One of these is Governor Lamar Alexander. His deputy, Tom Ingram, says, "Sure, Lamar understands the emotional appeal of George Wallace and Jesse Helms. But if you have a positive candidate who is good, who is intelligent and adroit, people will respond to him over a man who only tries to exploit social and economic problems. That's the kind of candidate who says, 'Yes, I'm mad, too, but here's what we can do about the problems we really can affect here in Tennessee.'" Right there in Tennessee Alexander's approach was approved by landslide proportions in his reelection bid in 1982. His brand of Republicanism is a welcome addition to statecraft in the South and could spell the end of the old personality politics of the Democratic South. That brand of politics can keep the southern electorate's attention focused on what we can do, here and now, to improve the possibilities of life after birth rather than guessing along with Helms about what lies in the conscience of the Almighty.

But Republicans will have a difficult time holding southern statehouses and gaining majorities in the region's legislatures until they begin to crack the Democrats' hold on the black vote. Alexander improved his appeal to black voters but still got only 15 to 20 percent. The Voting Rights Act of 1965 increased the number of black officeholders but had unintended consequences for southern GOP politics. In 1965 there were only 72 black elected officials in the 11 states of the Old Confederacy; by 1981, there were 2,535. Black political clout, however, is an obstacle to the Republican Party's growth in the South. The Voting Rights Act killed racial politics. But the civil rights movement died, too, which meant the end of a black community that was a moral monolith. Where there once was a religious crusade that united blacks of all ages, income, and political temperament, there is now a classical interest group with its own economic and political agenda. That agenda is a closer fit with the agenda of the Democratic Party. Political allegiances do not transfer overnight, so Democrats are likely to benefit from black support for a long time. President Reagan's benign neglect of the black agenda—or pernicious neglect, as most black leaders see it—makes it doubly difficult for moderate Republicans to broaden their base of appeal. In fact, the most significant question that may have been posed by Republican reversals in 1982 is this: can Republican presidential candidates continue to take the South for granted?

Which brings us to presidential politics in the South. The story rightly begins in 1970, the first political harvest from the seed of the Voting Rights Act of 1965. The "ABC" governors of the "new South" were all members of the class of '70: Reubin Askew of Florida, Dale Bumpers of Arkansas, and Jimmy Carter of Georgia. Until then, public men of the South were required to do the work of Sisyphus: rolling the scornful rock of poverty, pellagra, and prejudice up the hill. After the ABC governors, that kind of grunt-work wasn't needed any more. The men who succeeded them from both parties were of similar quality: Lamar Alexander of Tennessee, George Busbee of Georgia, Bill Clinton of Arkansas, Bob Graham of Florida, Jim Hunt of North Carolina, Dick Riley of South Carolina, Chuck Robb of Virginia, David Treen of Louisiana, and Bill Winter of Mississippi. But the people of the South needed a more visible sign from the nation before believing that Sisyphus's work had been done and that the South could come home as a respected partner. Then, on the morning of November 3, 1976, people awoke to the startling realization that the rock was gone; Sisyphus had been retired. The nation had elected a president from the Georgia Blackbelt: Jimmy Carter. The South had been affirmed, validated, inspected, and stamped U.S. Prime, 100-percent American. It was a time to whoop it up, to shout hallelujah and hear the echoes coming back from the amen corner. But you can't keep a good party going forever. Cultural joy begins to burn out at the moment of ecstasy.

I felt the first cold splash of reality in the Oval Office a few months after President Carter's inauguration. I was chatting with Jody Powell when I heard the president's familiar voice behind me. "Hello, Brandt," he said. "How's the South?" It was an offhand remark, as if he were inquiring about some place he had visited once or twice during the campaign. But it was a natural question. We didn't elect him to be president of the Confederacy. We chose him to be president of the United States of America, that unique office that is part prime minister, part king. Jimmy Carter is a man of simplicity and well-organized intelligence, wonderfully equipped to be prime minister or Senate majority leader, where the highest political skill is the politics of patience. But we didn't want a prime minister to talk to us, in the tedious, wooden words of policy, about issues beyond our comprehension or ability to affect. We wanted the president to speak to us in that other role, that of the elected American sovereign: symbol of our national virtues, the personification of the best in our national character, as the indispensable author of the national vision and the only man who can describe the nation's purpose and summon the national will. Jimmy Carter could not find the words that assembled many promising policies into a single picture in the mind of the republic, which also got in touch with the feelings of Americans. Lacking a structure of economic hope to present to the voters, he ran a negative campaign that made him seem peevish and small alongside the composed, good-humored, and confident Ronald Reagan. Governors who had served with Carter, some who had followed him, and even his close adviser, Jody Powell, agree that Carter's failure was a failure of articulation. That is a failure of leadership, despite Powell's emotionally compelling benediction: "Of course," he says, "but I grew up in those lost, good days when it was still more important to play a good game than it was to talk one."

There is another and perhaps dominant reason why the first president to be elected from the South since Zachary Taylor was rejected four years later by the nation and the South. He had terrible luck. The Iranian revolution frustrated national pride with the captivity of the hostages, and the oil shortage sent a shock of inflation through the whole economy, ballooning prices of everything made with oil or moved by it. With some anger and a lingering sadness that a southerner had not performed up to expectations, the South watched the Carter-Reagan debates and, a week later, rejected Carter as did the rest of America. Does Carter's failure of luck and leadership mean the last of the southern presidents for another hundred years? Not in the opinion of one quintessential Yankee, Scotty Reston of the *New York Times*. "We need someone to take these horribly complex international economic problems and put them into simple words that the people will understand," he says. "Nobody seems to know how to use the lan-

guage anymore, but southerners talk better. No, I don't think Jimmy Carter blotted his copy book so badly that a southern candidate would be
eliminated from consideration."

By that he didn't mean just *any* southerner. The brief, undeclared can-
didacy of Dale Bumpers, senior U.S. Senator from Arkansas, is a case
in point. He didn't abort his campaign because he was dismissed by the
media as another one of those hopeless southern candidates. He decided
against making the race for a cluster of personal and pragmatic reasons,
high among them the daunting necessity to raise about $300,000 a month.
Indeed, the media found him "interesting," as network pro Sander Van-
ocur of ABC put it. Tom Winship, editor of the *Boston Globe*, found him
"the most refreshing candidate to emerge from the pack." The best in-
formed Democratic professional in the South and the most respected national political writer, David Broder of the *Washington Post*, agreed that
Bumpers was emerging from the second tier of candidates as a genuine
contender when he abruptly announced on April 6, 1983, that he was dropping out.

Why Bumpers and not the other two declared candidates from the
South, U.S. Senator Ernest ("Fritz") Hollings of South Carolina and former Florida Governor Reubin Askew? Arkansas isn't perceived as any less
southern than South Carolina or Florida. What made Bumpers interesting
outside his home state and region may suggest the vague profile for southern candidacies in the future. He was popular with his colleagues in the
national forum of the U.S. Senate and, at the same time, independent. His
colleagues voted him "most likely to succeed," because he was confident
without being insufferably cocky; he mastered the details of the legislation
he managed without becoming a grinding bore. He could do the unexpected without being erratic. His lonely liberal vote against an antibusing
resolution and lonely conservative vote against extending the deadline for
ratifying the ERA amendment were bound together by his own view of
the Constitution. These were among the qualities that moved the capitol
press corps to vote him one of the ten best senators, and they were intrigued by the ability of a man from the village of Charleston, Arkansas, to
strike responsive chords from audiences in California and Massachusetts.

Any southerner—like any native of any region—with similar qualities of mind, character, and personality stands a chance if his timing is right and he can raise the money. The numbers further enhance the possibility of a credible presidential challenge by a southerner with the right stuff. The South has 133 electoral votes compared to the next closest, the Midwest, which has 113. The East and Midwest lost 17 electoral votes in the 1980 census. The South gained 8.

But every culture is doomed to interpret the world through the distorting lens of its own historical experience, and a good deal of the southern experience has been scorn and rejection. Though John Glenn says to the South, "You're no longer seeking to enter the mainstream of America; you *are* the mainstream." Though the early front-runner, former Vice-President Walter F. Mondale, so assiduously courted the region that at least two southern governors named him as their preference in the late spring. Though the old injury has smoothly healed on the surface, southerners instinctively continue to rub the phantom pain. Even such a sophisticated and self-confident man as Florida Governor Bob Graham says a southern presidential bid "is a net plus but a close call."

Graham's friend, Reubin Askew, and his southern competitor, Ernest Hollings, both say they confront skepticism about a southerner's chances mainly among southerners themselves. Askew refuses to feed Southern self-doubt. He meets it head-on, with outrageous humor, before southern audiences. "Well, of course, you're right," he says. "The South *is* a pretty sorry place, and we don't have anything much to offer the nation. We're culturally barren and poor and prejudiced but only because we're dumb, lazy, no 'count, shiftless. . . ."

As laughter rises to greet the preposterous caricature he is drawing, defeatist self-images begin to dissipate. It would be just as preposterous to say that Askew can't govern America because he is southern as it would be to say that he most certainly will win the presidency because he is southern.

Political writers of the stature of David Broder don't scoff at the idea of another southerner winning the Democratic nomination and the presidency. Broder doesn't believe that a senator from Ohio (John Glenn) or from Colorado (Gary Hart) has any more authority to speak to the nation than one from Arkansas (Dale Bumpers) or South Carolina (Ernest Hollings). One thing is certain. There will be only one southern candidate in the race two weeks after the New Hampshire primary in 1984. He will be the winner of a cluster of primaries that week in Florida, Georgia, Alabama, and Mississippi. But any southerner starts with an equal chance, because the region is no longer in thrall to the mad distraction of race.

If the South's defining purpose is no longer overcoming prejudice and marketing poverty and pellagra in exchange for federal entitlements, what are we now? Is old Dixie dead, a goner? "As different as the problems and opportunities are for Shreveport and Charlotte, there is still an affinity, a sense of common purpose in the South," says Florida's Governor Graham. He's right; Dixie won't die as long as the congregation still knows the words to "Precious Memories" and "Shall We Gather at the River." That perfectly irrational sense of being southern will last as long as there are people to sing "We Shall Overcome" and "Dixie" and as long as there are parents and grandparents to invest those songs with meaning, to plant that original cluster of primitive feelings that define people and place. But what vision will replace the discarded mythologies of the past: the subtropical Camelot of the Old South, with graces for the few and grits for the rest, and that great party we threw in the 1970s, that festival of the integrated, urbanized New South? This is a troubling question of values and policy.

One place to look for answers is the Southern Growth Policies Board, a product of the fecund imagination of the region's most thoughtful governor of the 1960s, Terry Sanford, who later became president of Duke University. Much to Sanford's disappointment, the board lost its way and became little more than a Dixie defense league protecting the South against raids on the federal treasury by Yankee units like the Northeast-Midwest Congressional Caucus. Mississippi's Governor Winter and Florida's Governor Graham agreed with Sanford that skirmishing with the Frostbelt was political and, thus, a job for the politicians—governors, legislators, and congressional delegations. During his term as chairman of the SGPB, Winter returned the board to its original purpose: an institution that sought to fashion theory and ideas into practical policy. Graham, who succeeded Winter as chairman, is dealing with a heady agenda. He talks about a new mission for the nation's first educational common market, the Southern Regional Education Board—a mission to retool the educational system to meet the demands of a postindustrial world economy. In fact, says Graham, "We must put overall emphasis on the international dimensions of the South because of our small-scale export industry." And like the author of the original "New South," Henry Grady, a century earlier, Graham is concerned about the continuing capital shortage in the region. Capital decisions made in New York and Boston are not as likely to be as sensitive to regional needs as they would if made by loan officers in Charlotte or Atlanta. He sees interstate banking just ahead on the horizon and says that "in order to insure the survival of southern finance, we need to encourage interstate banking among southern states by interstate agreement."

This is bold thinking with mind-boggling implications for the South and the nation. The South's policy agenda is nothing short of an attempt to solve the riddle of modernity: how does a society extract the material benefits of growth without destroying its cherished values? Good minds are grappling with the mechanical, the policy aspects of that riddle—ensuring capital formation for the needs of the South through regional interstate banking. The spiritual, the value side of the question, isn't getting the same attention. What values guided the hearts and minds of investment bankers in their decisions to finance only huge capital structures in downtown Atlanta and, thus, to banish the human community from its center? Atlanta might as well be Detroit: shining fingers of finance stuck impudently toward heaven while, in the canyons far below, muggers take control nightly at eleven. Aren't better models for making money and preserving values to be found in Charleston and Savannah, cities where people live, enjoy the accidental encounters of community, and protect themselves from unwelcome strangers?

The new agenda of policy and values may not be as obvious as the one with which the southern Sisyphus struggled; however, that agenda is forming with some clarity in the minds of public men of the South. Political leaders of both parties who wish to lead the nation through the 1980s can get a fairly clear map of the issues before the region by consulting the mind and conscience of southern governors, senators, and even a handful of journalists. But how can candidates from outside the region get southerners to respond to them politically? How do they speak to the cultural mysteries—to George Wallace's self-respect issue and to the Jesse Helms flock making its way through the wilderness of moral decay back to peace in the valley at the foot of Waltons' Mountain? We are back to the original question: will the South succumb to a demagogic appeal to the touchy, defensive pride of rural and working-class whites and to the antiabortion, antihomosexual, proprayer agenda of some white evangelicals? Hardly. Blacks wouldn't vote for such a candidate unless his opposition was utterly indifferent or frightening to them. A demagogue would also offend the large minority of issue-oriented white voters in the university and knowledge-industry cities of the South. Wallace failed to carry that vote and thus lost Auburn, Birmingham, Huntsville, and Tuscaloosa in both the primary runoff and the general election. Helms failed to score in the 1982 elections in North Carolina.

Southerners are also Americans. The South, like any other region, will respond to a statesman who looks beneath the surface to discover the hidden realities, who tells the truth, and who offers a sensible economic program. As the decade of the 1980s approached middle age, Americans of all races and regions were looking for the truth and the way. Is it true that all the fear, pain, and shame of unemployment and recession can be blamed on President Carter or on President Reagan? Partisan accusations fall on deaf ears in the cafes, barbershops, and taverns of the land. No one nods his head and says, "Now ain't *that* the truth?" What is the way? Which past do we choose: a return to classical laissez-faire with supply-side Reaganomics or a return to the New Deal by raising from the dead the Reconstruction Finance Corporation to run the nation's economy from Washington? How will the presidential candidates find the truth and the way— by going to each of the unions and associations and other special interests and asking, "What do *you* want?" That is the path of Gulliver, with gigantic gullibility, lying down and asking all the Lilliputian interests to weave their tiny threads around him until he is thoroughly immobilized. America isn't likely to be inspired by a candidate who enjoys bondage and willingly seeks it. In every presidential campaign, Americans have looked for a credible leader who says, "This way. Follow me." Americans are more likely to respond to a candidate who goes to the interests—business, education, and labor—and says, "Give me your energy and your ideas so that we can create an economic partnership to put the nation back to work and lead the world out of recession." The presidential election process has always been a search for leadership whose policies also touch our patriotic feelings. We will recognize the voice when we hear it, as we did on January 20, 1961, when a new president challenged us: "And so, my fellow Americans, ask not what your country can do for you—ask what you can do for your country."

Southerners, who were Americans before they ever thought to be southerners, from whose soil sprang the men who cast the whole shape of American democracy, will respond like any other Americans. They will respond to a person who sees the hidden realities about us as people, who tells the truth about national and world economic distress and offers a sensible economic program. But one of the hidden realities of the South is a distinctiveness rooted in its history and in its historic search for self-respect. A national candidate—whether he comes from Ohio or Florida—who gives the basic Wallace and Helms constituency a more affirmative reason for self-respect, rooted in positive values, will be the voice we have longed to hear. He can create a political coalition beyond the wildest dreams of Dr. King, the populists, or Franklin Roosevelt.

A New Culture Emerges in the Oil Patch

WILLIAM K. STEVENS

For a pilgrim westbound across the Deep South, to reach New Orleans and the Mississippi has always been to enter a different world. But today it is not so much the remnants of the old city's European culture or the city's neighbors, the Cajuns, that make the crucial difference. It is oil. More than anything else, oil and natural gas constitute the basic bonds that today hold the western half of the Sunbelt together, at once helping to define it as a distinct region of the United States and setting in motion economic and social forces that are reshaping its character and its outlook. New Orleans is the eastern gateway to the region, Los Angeles its land's end, Houston its de facto capital. These three cities are tied together by a steadily rising interchange of people, money, ideas, customs, popular pursuits, and political preferences. For lack of a better name, the region might be called the Oil Patch, after the driller's term for his own rough slice of turf, wherever it may lie. It is set off almost as distinctly from the Southeast as from the Northeast, even while it draws some of its values and thinking from both of those regions. The economic and social currents running within the region make Houston, for example, as different from Atlanta, in some ways, as it is from New York.

It is obviously true that New Orleans and Los Angeles are different from Houston and from each other, even through they are strongly linked in energy matters and in countless other ways. The Sunbelt is not of a single piece. New Orleans continues to hold much in common with the Southeast; and the sheer size and diversity of Los Angeles make it much more than the westernmost outpost of the Oil Patch in the same way that Chicago, although a part of the midwestern industrial crescent, is a world city in its own right. Still, commonalities seem to set off the vast sweep from Southern Louisiana to Southern California as a coherent region of the country. In addition, smaller cities on the periphery of the region, such as Tulsa and Oklahoma City and Hobbs, New Mexico, have long been drawn into the region's orbit. Now, mostly since 1970, Denver too has become an oil center and has thereby established strong economic and social connections to the Oil Patch. In fact, it might fairly be said that to the extent that the nation is regionally divided today, it is not along north-south lines but along east-west ones. The crux of the division is energy. Take away oil and gas, and the Oil Patch would subside into something far less vital than it has lately become, something far less likely to excite the economic envy of the East.

Within this churning region a new middle-class culture is taking shape. It is distinct from anything that has preceded it, yet it owes its nature to many ancestors. It is displayed in perhaps its most clearly defined form in the urban "core" of Texas—that is, the big triangle, roughly two hundred miles on a side, that connects Houston, San Antonio, and Dallas-Fort Worth. This is an area that was settled in the last century mainly by southerners from the East, settlers whose customs, values, and speech clearly stamped Texas as a part, or at least an offshoot, of the Old South. Those strains are still strongly evident; but today they are challenged, diffused, modified, and increasingly blurred by a rich variety of other kinds of people and outlooks, many of them strong-willed migrants from Yankeeland. As is true elsewhere, this change is happening at a time when the moderating influences of literacy, mass communications, and easy travel have rubbed the edges off the regional idiosyncracies of earlier days.

It seems appropriate to focus initially on Texas. It is the geographic heart and technological center of the Oil Patch, and the region's characteristics are displayed there in most undiluted form. Moreover, Texas is the cultural and economic mediator between Louisiana on the east and Southern California on the west. For all its early history as an independent nation and its well-known fierce sense of identity and uniqueness, Texas has in many ways been a creature of the earlier American South. The influences of Spain and Mexico on the state are well known and—because of rising Mexican-American birth rates and a swelling flood of immigration from Mexico—becoming stronger all the time. Furthermore, significant numbers of northern European immigrants, Germans and Czechs foremost among them, came to Texas during the nineteenth century. But the dominant influence in the state's formation was southeastern: southern values, customs, and speech characterized the Anglo pioneers who took the state away from Mexico and began to exploit its land and resources. For a long time the economic results of that conquest remained unspectacular. Texas was mostly a land of small farms and small farmers, and despite the rise of cattle barons after the Civil War, it remained a hardscrabble country much like the Southeast. It escaped the physical devastation that the Southeast suffered, and for that reason refugees from the Deep South flocked to resettle in Texas after the war. But Texas remained a relatively poor land and was viewed in northern eyes as an exotic but backward province.

Spindletop, in 1901, along with the advent of the mass-produced automobile a few years later, signaled the eventual end of Texas's days as a poor relative of the North—and as a psychological appendage of the Old South. The discovery of the world's first megadeposit of oil at Spindletop, near Beaumont, launched Texas on a course that over the next eighty years would enable the state to pull even with the nation as a whole in per-capita wealth. After World War II, it would convert the Lone Star State into a full-fledged, urbanized entity that could legitimately aspire to play in the big leagues with California and New York, the only two states that in 1982 were more populous than Texas.

It is both Texas's fortune and its misfortune to be viewed in mythical terms. From the real cowboys of a century ago to the urban cowboys of today, Texas's tall-in-the-saddle legend has made a unique claim on the world's imagination. The only trouble is that the legend has obscured present-day reality. The reality is that Texas has become sophisticated and diversified, even though its economy continues to be based on energy and agribusiness; that a matching diversity and sophistication is taking place socially; and that 80 percent of Texans, or more, are urban dwellers. Some Texans who prize the old ways fear that in the rush to join the national leagues, Texas is losing much that is distinctive. They are probably right. Old Texas, like the Old South of which it was once a part, is disappearing. As middle-class migrants from the North flood into the north-side suburbs of Dallas and San Antonio and into the west side of Houston, as Mexican nationals swell the barrios of those cities, as Asians and others migrate to Texas in search of opportunity, the old ways become more and more submerged.

But not entirely. The new society is often as segregated as the old one ever was. In Houston, for instance, the Mexican-American barrios and black ghettos of the east side may as well be on a different planet from the comfortable, tree-shaded precincts of the upper-middle-class west side, a kind of conservative Camelot-on-the-Bayou. Economic divisions are wide, too, wider than in the northern United States. At least one study has shown that the affluent of Texas get a proportionately larger slice of the pie than they do nationally, while the poor get a proportionately smaller slice. Unemployment rates in the oil cities have been ridiculously low in northern eyes, but this is misleading: because of low wage scales, there are hundreds of thousands of working poor. Nor is the wealth well distributed geographically. In virtually every case, the prosperous Texas cities are based on oil. Cities that don't have oil economies, such as those in the Rio Grande Valley, are among the nation's poorest. In the affluent Camelots of Dallas, San Antonio, Houston, Austin, Lubbock, Midland, and Amarillo, however, a new hybrid suburban society of the western Sunbelt is emerging in a setting of sleek brick homes, airy, glass-walled contemporaries, and interestingly angled town houses that have sprung out of the hills and prairies and rice fields and piney woods just since 1960. It is a world populated by risk-taking entrepreneurs; by middle- and upper-level managers, white-collar workers, oil-company executives, geologists, and others associated with the oil industry; by bankers and financiers and developers and businessmen of every description; and by professionals—from physicians to architects to artists to musicians—who have gravitated to what they perceive to be the land of opportunity. In this world, the flood of middle-class migration from the North has come to rest.

The new society that is emerging in this world is neither traditionally Texan nor traditionally Yankee. It is something all its own. The emerging diversity is changing the accent and food of Houston. Afghan, Vietnamese, Moroccan, Lebanese, Russian, Thai, Indian, Ethiopian, Cajun, and Cuban restaurants now vie with Mexican food and barbecue, and the workman in your house is as likely to be a white ethnic from Michigan humming an aria from an opera as a good ole boy from rural Texas with a slow Dixie drawl. The perspective of the new society is national and, thanks to the influence of the worldwide energy industry, international as well. Its outlook is conservative, but with a strong streak of pragmatic moderation. In some households it also displays a strong streak of redneck racism, modified only slightly by the split-level, button-down environment. In others, the atmosphere is one of racial and ethnic tolerance—up to a point. On balance, one gets the sense that as middle-class Texas has gotten more diverse and sophisticated, it has become more tolerant as well.

And, like the state as a whole, it has become more independent politically. The new Texas independents have been identified as the pivotal group in the state's politics. With the election of William P. Clements in 1978 as the first Republican governor of Texas since Reconstruction, it was widely said that Texas had at last become a two-party state. No longer, analysts said, did conservative Democrats dominate the state, as they once had the entire Southland. In those days of Democratic dominance, Republicans were a fringe group. Liberal Democrats made a lot of noise, occasionally swung some weight, and from time to time elected candidates. But generally they either had to play ball with the entrenched conservatives of their party or become ineffectual. With the rise of the new Texas Camelot, the Republicans saw a potential constituency that might enable them, at last, to become a truly competitive force. Clements helped prove it by riding to victory, largely in the Camelot precincts. Since then, Republicans have made further gains. They have a strong party organization. But they are not dominant. Neither, any longer, are the Democrats. Surveys show that neither party has a strong enough hold on enough of the electorate to achieve dominance. The independents hold the balance.

Who are the independents? Political analysts have identified three main groups. First, there are the Yankee Republicans, migrants from the Northeast, the Midwest, or California. Second, there are the college-educated sons and daughters of the Texas countryside and small towns, raised as Democrats, who have now moved to Camelot and taken their place in the affluent society. One such Texan, an oil-company executive in his mid-forties who grew up in the small town of Temple but now lives on Houston's glossy northwest side, put it this way: "When I first came to Houston, I hadn't seen more than three Yankees in my whole life. Now I deal with them all the time, and it's changed me, just by the association of it, and I think it's changed them, too. I guess I felt inferior in a way. The message I got initially was that they didn't feel like we could run on the same track that they ran on." Now, he says, he knows he can run on that track. Multiply that by hundreds of thousands, and a major shift in regional perception may have taken place. The psychosocial consequences of such a shift could be incalculable. Politically, it seems to bolster a growing feeling of independence. The third element of the new Texas Middle, or independent segment of the electorate, consists of a slightly older group of people, perhaps fifty-five to sixty years old, who have stayed in the small towns of West Texas but shifted away from a come-what-may allegiance to the Democratic party. These new independents tend to vote Republican, since their bent is basically conservative, and especially so on economic questions. But they will not necessarily do so. They are said to be more interested in issues and personalities than in party, and they hold the new balance of power in the state's politics. Because of them, Texas has been called a "no-party" state.

Historically, despite a strong liberal-populist minority tradition, Texas has never been much different from the rest of the South in its attitude toward racial minorities. That is changing, too, at least insofar as Mexican-Americans are concerned. Power elites in cities large and small have lately been forced to come to grips with the aspirations of Hispanic voters. Initially, amendments to the Voting Rights Act forced them to. Under the amendments, cities were forced to restructure their city council elections so as to reflect approximately the ethnic makeup of their communities. The result was that in Houston, Dallas, and San Antonio, Texas's three largest cities, blacks and Mexican-Americans for the first time obtained a share of governing power that was long denied them. In the spring of 1981 San Antonio, where Mexican-Americans now constitute a majority of the population, elected the first Mexican-American mayor of a major American city in modern times. Henry Cisneros, thirty-three years old, won with a smashing 62 percent of the vote, and the fact that he nearly carried the Camelot precincts of the north side—an unheard-of feat in earlier years—is a measure of the change in attitudes there. Republican governor Clements lost, and by a surprisingly wide margin, to Democrat Mark White in 1982, a result of the deepening recession in a Texas that had often bragged about being recession-proof, and of Clements's image as tough-talking, arrogant, and uncaring. Moreover, Clements had irritated women, blacks, Mexicans, and many average consumers of electricity who saw White as caring more about middle-class and lower-income Texans.

All of this is part of a general moderation of the basic political climate that seems to be taking place in Texas. Growth at any cost, preached and advocated in a no-compromise, hard-nosed manner, has seemed to be the state's philosophy in recent years. Now, in Houston at least, movers and shakers are more than beginning to talk about controlling growth, about slowing annexation, about a breathing spell in which the infrastructure of city services, inadequate in some places, can catch up with development. Indeed, the 1979 mayor's race in Houston was fought on just such issues, and many candidates who favored a more rational approach to growth were elected. Kathy Whitmire's whopping victory in the 1981 mayoral election was a resounding vote for better management, better governmental services, better control of growth. This doesn't mean that the advocates of growth have disappeared, or even that they no longer predominate. Growth is still strong, still fed by the optimism that a booming economy breeds. It is simply being reined in somewhat.

As Southern Louisiana has come to share the same oil boom that fuels Texas's prodigious growth, Texas attitudes have invaded the bayous and even established more than a beachhead in New Orleans. In recent years Louisiana public officials have been preaching free enterprise, industrial development, growth, and change. This has led some in New Orleans to fear that their city was becoming "Houstonized." It might seem that way, what with the Superdome, the sterile skyscraper of One Shell Square—a virtual twin of Houston's One Shell Plaza—looming over the Vieux Carré, and whole colonies of oil-company executives, some of them transplanted directly from Houston, living on the West Bank. With its big Shell refinery, the town of Norco, just up the river from New Orleans, is a dead ringer for the refinery-lined banks of the Houston Ship Channel. Move out into the countryside, and the theme holds. Acadiana is now known as much for its drilling rigs and production platforms as for its crawfish and pirogues, and many a Cajun lets his joie de vivre run loose at night after having worked as a roughneck by day. Lafayette, the center of both Acadiana and the Louisiana stretch of the Oil Patch, seems almost as full of former Texans as it is of Louisianans. Perhaps the most popular eating place in Lafayette, where Cajun cooking has long been supreme, is a Mexican restaurant run by a man who came from San Antonio. It is not as if Texas were colonizing Louisiana. For one thing, Texans who move to Louisiana are more likely to be converted to that state's traditionally graceful, slower way of life than to subvert it. It is rather like Rome's subversion by Greek thought and ways. For another thing, not all the social and economic currents run east. They also run west. Red beans and rice, jambalaya, and oyster "po-boy" sandwiches are almost as easy to find in Houston as in Louisiana. Cajuns abound in Houston, and the country-and-western radio stations regularly play Cajun music. It is just one more element in the tangy, cosmopolitan texture that is coming to characterize Houston. Lastly, the era of jet flight and of the interstate highway has made it easy to travel between New Orleans and Houston. It is a six-hour drive and a forty-five-minute flight. Businessmen, particularly those in oil and gas, move between Texas and Louisiana so routinely that it is almost like commuting. Even impulse travel in both directions by those seeking a weekend of fun and relaxation or shopping is common.

Still more elements are added to the rich new social and economic mixture of the evolving Oil Patch as a result of the Texas-California connection. Texas and California appear to be linked ever more strongly by a variety of common interests and affinities, to such a degree that an unacknowledged power alliance is developing between them, similar to the one that developed between New York and Chicago a century ago. This time the economic ties consist not of rails, wheat, and heavy industry, but of oil, space-age technology, petrochemicals, cross-border real estate activity, and—most important, perhaps, in terms of social and cultural change—waves of migrants and visitors who move back and forth between the two states. Just as manufacturing defined the cities of the Northeast during the nineteenth century, so Texas and Southern California are being jointly defined, in large measure, by energy production, agriculture, high technology, and military activity, by middle-class lifestyles and values that seem increasingly interchangeable, and by the large and growing presence of Mexican-Americans. The affinities are apparent even in the look of things: except that Southern California's landscape is far more beautiful, Los Angeles and Houston could be urban brothers, so similar are their dispersed patterns of development, their freeway systems, their far-flung suburbs, and their downtown skyscrapers. Just as New Orleans has One Shell Square and Houston has One Shell Plaza, so Los Angeles's skyline would not be complete without the Arco Tower—nor its economy without oil and gas. After Texas, Alaska, and Louisiana, California ranks fourth in oil production in the United States. As might be expected, this leads to a considerable interchange of people between Southern California and Texas, just as it does between Texas and Louisiana.

That is just the beginning. The great surge of post–World War II westing migration has now bounced off the West Coast and ricocheted back to Texas. California's higher living costs, diminishing opportunities in a more mature economy, increasing scarcity of usable land at reasonable prices, growing governmental restrictions, and no-growth ethic have all combined to send increasing numbers of Californians looking to the next big, relatively wide-open, unfettered land of opportunity. For many that means Texas. Both money and people are making the trip. Calfornia capital that once would have fueled the growth of, say, the San Fernando Valley, is now pouring into Texas real estate developments. And the available statistics indicate that California is second only to Louisiana in the number of new residents it sends to Houston. Texas is in some ways the new California. As was true twenty to thirty years ago on the "Left Coast," as some Texans call it, there is an apparent loosening of traditional values and lifestyles in Texas. By no stretch of the imagination is it the experimental laboratory that California is, but the Californians who migrate to Texas are unavoidably taking some of the values of Lotus Land with them. In some cases that might not be much of a switch. Politically, for instance, there is a marked affinity between many conservative middle-class residents of Southern California and conservative middle-class Texans. The winning presidential – vice-presidential ticket of California's Ronald Reagan and Texas's George Bush symbolizes the emergence of this cross-state constituency beautifully. But in other ways, the California-to-Texas migrants could have a loosening-up effect on a state once dominated by Baptist morality; middle-class Houstonians as a group still "don't allow the deviations [in behavior] that they allow in California," said one recent Los Angeles-to-Houston migrant.

There is middle-class migration the other way, too, from Texas to California; but because today's economic conditions tend to favor it less, it does not appear to be as heavy as in the California-to-Texas direction. For this reason, and also because Texan influences tend to get swallowed up in the overwhelming, cosmopolitan variety of Southern California, the long-term impact of the Texas-California interchange on values and the shaping of culture probably will be greater in Texas than on the West Coast.

Will Texas, once the western anchor of the Old South, become, in the phrase of Texas-born novelist Larry McMurtry, "a sort of kid brother to California, with a kid brother's tendency to imitation?" Possibly, but not likely. Too many other influences are being brought to bear in Texas today. Too many people from many other states are moving in, especially from midwestern industrial states like Michigan. In addition, the cowboy hats, jeans, and boots that are favored by many urban Texans who have never set foot on the range are not totally frivolous. They symbolize traditional Texan ways of looking at the world, attitudes that were developed by the nineteenth-century pioneers. Those values remain very much alive. Independence of thought and action, directness, and self-reliance are not merely ideals for Texans of the 1980s. They are instincts for many who remember grandparents who actually lived on the frontier. They suit the predilections of many conservative, middle-class migrants from elsewhere. And they seem certain to work their influence for at least a while.

Beyond that, only time will reveal the still-coalescing shape of the Oil Patch culture. The rise of the Mexican-Americans, their aspirations, and their claim to a rightful place in the southwestern sun will determine much about the region's future. In time, the Oil Patch itself is likely to decline economically as oil and natural gas reserves are depleted. The region received a foretaste of what this might mean, perhaps, when world oil prices dropped sharply in 1982, dimming the sheen of the gilt-edged Oil Patch economy somewhat and sending nervous tremors through the middle-class dwellers of Camelot. How they respond to the challenges that certainly lie in the future will largely set the tone and determine the direction of this new American power bloc. One thing seems certain: however the region's economy and social profile evolve, the future will be very different from the past as vestiges of the Old South grow ever fainter.

☆ ☆ ☆ **9** ☆ ☆ ☆

The Sunbelt

JAMES R. ADAMS

In the last half of the 1970s "the South" almost seemed to disappear. This term, so redolent of history and tragedy, of blood and magnolias, merged into a regional label of new coinage: "the Sunbelt." That term originated with the demographers and economists. It drew its life from studies of population movement, plant location, personal income growth, and the like. The word, in short, was a statistical abstraction, even a statistical myth. It did reflect one very important development in the fourteen-state South.[1] For the first time since the Civil War this region was winning its struggle to catch up with the national economy. But it is an unanswered question whether the economic progress synonymous with the term "Sunbelt" has grown out of anything specifically southern in history, character, or even climate.

According to Professor George Brown Tindall,[2] the term first appeared

1. Virginia, West Virginia, Kentucky, Tennessee, North Carolina, South Carolina, Georgia, Florida, Alabama, Mississippi, Louisiana, Arkansas, Texas, Oklahoma. All definitions of the "South," let alone of the "Sunbelt," are arbitrary. The U. S. Department of Commerce divides these states between its Southeast and Southwest groupings. (The latter also includes Arizona and New Mexico.) The Census Bureau breaks them up into the South Atlantic (which also includes Maryland, Delaware, and the District of Columbia), East South Central, and West South Central.

2. George Brown Tindall, "The Sunbelt Snow Job," *Houston Review* 1 (Spring 1979): 3.

in the book, *The Emerging Republican Majority,*[3] written in 1969 by Kevin
P. Phillips, a native of New York City. Mr. Phillips, then special assistant to
U. S. attorney general John N. Mitchell, argued that American politics was
being transformed by the population and economic shift to the "sun country." His thesis, which now appears so prophetic, lay in eclipse for much of
the decade. The term was revived, says Professor Tindall, in the 1975 book,
*Power Shift: The Rise of the Southern Rim and Its Challenge to the Eastern
Establishment.*[4] This book was the work of the New Left writer Kirkpatrick
Sale, a native of Ithaca, New York. It should be a sign of caution that the
description was first applied from outside the region and that both writers
stretched the idea to include California, which is a separate economic empire with its own bizarre and fascinating history.

   Southern boosters had good reason not to debunk the phrase, however,
since it became one of the best selling points they had ever had. In 1977, for
instance, a trade mission from the Houston Chamber of Commerce arrived in Japan to find that Sale's book had been translated into Japanese.
Although Mr. Sale had written a polemic filled with derogatory remarks
about "Rimster cowboys," the Japanese read it eagerly as a guidebook to
the newest area of economic growth. The Houston delegation found Japanese corporations clamoring to get in on the ground floor.[5]

   For all its usefulness in chamber-of-commerce propaganda, the word
"Sunbelt" is a very misleading overgeneralization. It implies a homogeneous region of uniform economic growth. Yet the fourteen-state South
contains at least three or four (and more likely up to fourteen) distinctive
economies. Juan de Torres of the Conference Board, a New York-based
business research organization, identifies three main subsections: a manufacturing crescent from Richmond, Virginia, through the Carolinas and
Georgia to Birmingham, Alabama; the resort-and-retirement-oriented
Florida peninsula; and the Gulf, dominated by Houston. But he consigns
West Virginia, Kentucky, and most of Tennessee to the Midwest and most

   3. Kevin P. Phillips, *The Emerging Republican Majority* (New York: Arlington House,
1969).

   4. Kirkpatrick Sale, *Power Shift: The Rise of the Southern Rim and Its Challenge to the
Eastern Establishment* (New York: Vintage Books, 1976).

   5. Conversation with Houston Chamber of Commerce officials.

of Texas and Oklahoma to the Southwest.[6] Alternatively, one could separate out the "oil states" of Louisiana, Texas, and Oklahoma, a region that the *Congressional Quarterly* depicts as a separate grouping on its national political map and that William K. Stevens calls the "oil patch." To the extent that their state budgets and economies depend on a tight market in oil and natural gas, these states sometimes have more in common with OPEC than with the rest of the South.

These subregions, furthermore, operate on separate economic rhythms. The "manufacturing crescent" swings even more widely than the rest of the country through the ups and downs of the national business cycle. Florida has suffered its own boom and bust, intensified by speculative overbuilding. Until the oil glut of 1981–1982 lowered both prices and output, the "oil patch" had been riding a seemingly endless boom. In the national recession from January to July of 1980, nine states of the Sunbelt-South performed significantly more poorly than the national average; four other Sunbelt states (Florida and the oil bloc) had the highest growth rates in the country. The disparity was even more dramatic in the recession of 1981–1982 (or, as some called it, the 1981–1982 continuation of the 1980 recession). The East-South-Central region of Kentucky, Tennessee, Mississippi, and Alabama was the second most hard-hit in the country. In March 1982 Alabama soared into the unenviable position of having the nation's second-highest unemployment rate.[7]

Although rapid immigration and population growth are in the popular mind almost the defining characteristics of the Sunbelt, the overwhelming bulk of this population shift has taken place in just two states, Texas and Florida. The term "Sunbelt" triggers one final and very unfortunate stereotype in northeastern minds. This is the notion, as New York mayor Edward Koch is fond of putting it, that "the South is getting rich, and we are getting poor." In fact, as all the figures indicate clearly, what has transpired

6. Juan de Torres, "The New South: The Sunbelt May be Cooling Slightly," *Across the Board* (March 1977): 4–11.

7. Robert Bretzfelder and Howard Friedenberg, "State Personal Income, Second Quarter, 1980," *Survey of Current Business* (Bureau of Economic Analysis, U. S. Department of Commerce, October 1980): 18–19; Bureau of Economic Analysis, May 9, 1982; U. S. Department of Labor, *Employment and Earnings* (May 1980).

is a narrowing of the great disparity among regional per capita incomes, but with remarkably little change in the regional order of ranking. At the turn of the century, per capita income in the Southeast was less than 50 percent of the national average; by the late 1970s, it had grown to 86 percent. Yet the Southeast still has the lowest per capita income in the country. The Northeast has complained vociferously about its declining relative position, yet since the turn of the century the biggest loser, at least statistically, has been California.[8] The rebuttal is that when the cost of living is factored in, the middle class in the Sunbelt comes out comfortably ahead of its northern counterpart. Supporting examples can readily be found, yet the question of regional cost-of-living variations has to be approached with caution. The Poverty Studies Task Force of the United States Department of Health, Education, and Welfare concluded in 1976 that "there is no known way to make satisfactory geographic adjustments" in the cost of living.[9] This index can vary widely between cities in the same region and state and even between a city and its surrounding countryside; such variations often exceed the variations between regions. Some crude attempts at such adjustments have, however, brought southwestern per capita income approximately to the national average and have shifted the Southeast from the poorest to the second poorest region (after New England). In the meantime, the "Frostbelt" seems oblivious to the irony that its conflict with the Sunbelt derives from their growing more alike.

In spite of these misconceptions, it is true that the Sunbelt has prospered in the 1970s. The pattern of national dispersion of the population and wealth and of economic convergence among regions, which has been traced from 1870, has indeed accelerated in the last decade. The popular explanations for this prosperity, however, are often as far off the mark as are the popular stereotypes of the Sunbelt.

One thesis especially favored by northern politicians holds that southern progress derives from a favorable balance in the federal flow of funds.[10]

8. Advisory Commission on Intergovernmental Relations, "Regional Growth: Historic Perspective," *Commission Report A-74* (June 1980): 12.

9. Quoted in ibid., p. 27, n. 1.

10. See, for instance, "Federal Spending: The Northeast's Loss is the Sunbelt's Gain," *National Journal* (June 1976).

This growing region, they maintain, has been receiving more in federal spending than it pays in federal taxes, while their own stagnating states have been paying more than they receive. Therefore, they conclude, this flow should be reversed to shore up the "declining" North. A superficial glance at the numbers shows that such discrepancies do exist. On average, the Southeast is the second-largest gainer (after the Far West); the Great Lakes region loses the most by far. But the conclusion that this flow has given the South an unfair advantage, or that the funds are even the cause of its growth, runs into serious problems in concept, fact, and equity.

The core of the flow-of-funds argument is a curiously medieval view of the national economy, in which the only commerce between regions takes place at the direction of the sovereign. In our massive, integrated national economy, it is frequently impossible to tell which is the source and which the final beneficiary of any federal fund. This confusion shows up in a difficulty with the data. The federal tax receipts from several states are clearly exaggerated by the presence of national headquarters of large corporations. These corporations pay taxes through a single location on profits they have earned throughout the country and world. This situation particularly applies in New York State, which its senator, Daniel Patrick Moynihan, has vigorously tried to portray as a victim of the "flow-of-funds." Two Columbia University researchers drew up six methods of allocating the true "flow-of-funds" balance, and found that for all but the most distorted formula New York State emerged a net gainer.[11] Furthermore, it is a historical fact that the flow-of-funds disparity has narrowed substantially in the twenty-five years since 1952. In 1952 the Southeast received $1.51 in federal spending for each dollar it paid in taxes, while the Mideast got back only 75¢; in 1976 the Southeast got back $1.11, and the Mideast received $1.02. The narrowing disparity reflects the narrowing in

11. Charles Brecher and Kurt W. Katzmar, "The Size and Nature of the Public Sector in New York City" (Paper delivered at Lehrman Institute Seminar on Local Government, January 26, 1978; available from the Lehrman Institute, 42 East 71st Street, New York, New York 10021), charts 1 and 2. A revised version was published as "An Unconventional Look at the Public Sector," *New York Affairs* 5 (Spring 1979): 29 ff., but without the charts. The paper is also discussed in Ken Auletta, *The Streets Were Paved with Gold* (New York: Random House, 1979), pp. 124–29.

the gap between regional incomes. According to research sponsored by the Advisory Commission on Intergovernmental Relations,[12] above-average collection in federal taxes is very closely tied to a state's above-average per capita income; but it is hard to show a strong correlation between a surplus in federal spending and growth in the personal income of a state's residents. Texas, for instance, is the first southern state to bring its per capita income above the national average, even in nominal dollars, and Houston has a very high per capita income. Yet it has been paying far more in federal taxes than it gets back in federal disbursements.

In short, the "flow-of-funds" argument describes the impact of a progressive national tax system on states with high incomes. The very point of a progressive tax is to make the rich pay proportionally more for services than the poor. For this reason, leaders in some wealthy states, such as then-governor Charles Evans Hughes of New York, opposed the original adoption of the federal income tax. The flow-of-funds issue would make sense as a renewed attack on the progressive income tax, but such an aim is hard to find stated explicitly; and many of the issue's most enthusiastic advocates would undoubtedly be horrified to find themselves headed in that direction.

Another popular explanation for southern growth has been its climate, although this thesis may seem more plausible to an editorial writer in New York than to a summer pedestrian in Houston. One may conclude that people will migrate to escape the harsh northeast and north-central winters without necessarily admitting that they will wind up in the heat of the Gulf Coast. In terms of a low average of combined heating and cooling degree days, the most attractive region is the Pacific Coast.[13] This explanation may also have validity for Florida, but it seems an overgeneralization to apply it too heavily to the rest of the Sunbelt-South. In fact, one variation of the theme maintains that the Sunbelt was really opened to economic growth by the advent of air conditioning. Yet air conditioning imposes an energy cost on both businesses and residents. Because of peculiarities in utility

12. ACIR, "Regional Growth," pp. 62 ff.
13. Lynn E. Browne, "The Shifting Pattern of Interregional Migration," *New England Economic Review* (November/December 1979): 27.

regulation and fuel supply, this cost has become extraordinarily high in places like San Antonio, Texas, which nevertheless continue to receive some of the highest proportions of immigration in the Sunbelt.

These arguments have recently encountered another serious difficulty. Although climate remains a constant, the pattern of regional growth has been shifting. In the first quarter of 1980 New England had the highest personal income increase in the country, in the middle of exceptionally harsh weather. In March 1982 the state with the highest growth rate east of the Mississippi was New Hampshire, whose cold winters are legend, and its 10 percent increase in personal income over the year was exceeded in the Sunbelt only by Texas.[14]

Residents of the South explain its growth more plausibly in terms of its "pro-business" attitude. Great efforts have gone into luring corporations from the North with tax exemptions, municipal financing, and other industrial inducements. Yet the migrating corporate headquarters is a relatively rare phenomenon. Only a fraction of the region's growth can be attributed to such a relocation, and those that have occurred have been concentrated disproportionately in Houston, which holds a unique position in the Sunbelt as the world center of petroleum technology. An impressive body of evidence casts doubt on the weight that corporations give to governmental inducements in their decisions to locate.[15] Except for competition among nearby sites, businessmen are more concerned about their needs for transportation, market access, raw materials, and the amenities of life. Other Sunbelt talking points also carry their drawbacks. The promise of "cheap labor" implies the lack of a highly skilled labor force and may repel the kind of sophisticated enterprise that can achieve the highest rate of growth. One frequently hears that, with action by Louisiana in 1976, all fourteen southern states now have "right-to-work" laws. This argument has the same kind of superficial plausibility for a southern conservative that the flow-of-funds thesis holds for a northern liberal. Relatively weak unions do lessen business costs, although more through a greater

14. *Business Week*, July 26, 1982.

15. See Roger J. Vaughn, *State Taxation and Economic Development* (Washington, D. C.: Council of State Planning Agencies, 1979), pp. 3–8, 95–112.

flexibility in work rules than through lower wages. Yet, as we shall explain, "right-to-work" laws are more significant as a symptom of a political attitude rather than as a direct cause of growth. If overemphasized, they may detract attention from the real roots of southern prosperity.

Perhaps the best way to present our explanation of the Sunbelt is to solve the riddle of Louisiana. This fascinating state commands the second largest reserves of oil and natural gas in the lower forty-eight states. It boasts a most charming commercial metropolis that sits astride a major transportation route to the American heartland and offers one of the busiest water ports in the country. Yet until the mid-1970s it lagged while the rest of the Sunbelt bustled. Although its hourly wage rates in manufacturing remained well above the regional average from 1960 to 1970, its rate of growth in nonagricultural employment was the third worst in the region. During this decade the average annual per capita income growth in the Southeast was 120 percent of the U. S. average. But the growth in Louisiana was only 108 percent of the national average, the lowest in the region.

Around 1975 this pattern reversed itself. The average hourly manufacturing wage grew even further above the regional average and in fact exceeded the national average by more than 6 percent. But far from hurting the state's competitive position, this high wage scale went hand in hand with a remarkable acceleration of the state's economic growth. From 1974 to 1981 Louisiana's per capita personal income soared from 79 percent of the national average to 90 percent. Over the decade from 1970 to 1980, its increase in this measure was matched only by that of Texas and Oklahoma. The next most successful southeastern state, Virginia, bettered its standing by only 6 percentage points. The difference was even more pronounced in the 1980–1982 recession. From 1978 to 1981, Louisiana's per capita personal income grew 42.5 percent, a rate 18 percent higher than the nation's and 17 percent higher than the Southeast's. In the nation, only Texas, Oklahoma, and Connecticut did better.[16]

The natural rejoinder is that this growth came about almost exclusively

16. Bretzfelder and Friedenberg, "1980 State Per Capita Income" (Bureau of Economic Analysis publication no. 81-25, May 3, 1981); "Fourth Quarter 1981 State Nonfarm Personal Income and 1981 State Per Capita Personal Income" (BEA publication no. 82-83, May 9, 1982).

because of the oil boom in the Southwest caused by the 1973–1974 Arab oil embargo. This argument has more than a surface plausibility. In 1973, Louisiana's oil and gas production generated severance tax receipts of $265 million. In 1975 these receipts had more than doubled, to $546 million. Yet the argument overlooks the self-defeating nature of American energy policy in the 1970s. Federal price controls quickly limited the benefits that domestic producers might have realized from further world price increases. Severance tax receipts actually declined in each of the next four years, falling to $466 million in 1979. Since some price increases had taken place, moreover, these figures mask an even sharper decline in oil and natural gas production. The real petroleum turnaround came in 1981, long after Louisiana's economic boom was an established fact.[17]

A large component of this boom was unquestionably the petroleum and petrochemical industry, yet oil prices alone cannot account for the state's 24 percent increase in nonagricultural employment from 1976 to 1981. (The comparable U. S. increase was only 14 percent.) Although the highest percentage increase (56 percent) came in mining, the U. S. Department of Labor classification that includes oil and gas drilling, the figure numerically translates into only 35,000 jobs. By contrast, the service and wholesale and retail trade sectors added 129,000 jobs in this period, more than 40 percent of the total gain. Another 30 percent of the increase came in the categories of finance, insurance, and real estate; transportation and public utilities; and government, a total of 95,800 jobs. In short, 70 percent of the boom in Louisiana's work force came in areas not directly related to hydrocarbons.[18] One can argue, of course, that this increased activity reflects the "multiplier effect" of oil and gas income, a point reinforced by the distribution of growth within the state. The most populous parishes, those around Shreveport, Baton Rouge, the "river parishes" upstream and downstream from New Orleans, and those along the Gulf Coast, are also centers of hydrocarbon production and processing. Yet these areas have also begun to attract other types of construction and manufacturing—a steel mill,

17. Figures from Louisiana Department of Revenue.

18. U. S. Department of Labor, *Employment and Earnings* (October 1978); ibid. (May 1982).

some high technology—even though in the preceding paragraph I arbitrarily assigned the growth in these two sectors to the petroleum boom. A more precise question to ask would be why Louisiana suddenly began to attract industrial investment and immigration after a period in which both had shunned the state. According to the Louisiana Association of Business and Industry, the state received more in industrial investment from 1975 to 1980 ($10.5 billion) than it had in the previous fifteen years. In the same five-year span, its population grew by 8 percent, compared to an average of 6 percent over the preceding three five-year periods. In spite of the increased value of the state's natural resources, its exploiters retain the option of developing that wealth within the state or exporting it for processing elsewhere, as Louisianians have maintained that national corporations were doing for most of the twentieth century.[19]

It appears that more of the wealth is staying within the state now, and Louisianians offer several reasons based on their own changes in state policy. LABI argues that passage of right-to-work legislation in 1976 made the difference, as the symbol of a much more pro-business political climate. Reformers cite a noticeable (but not universal) diminution of corruption and rejuvenation of political behavior. However, our interest is in the state's tax policy. As a general topic of inquiry, this area offers insights, not only into the economic performance of Louisiana, but into that of the Sunbelt and of the fifty states altogether. It also has bearing on the national debate on "supply-side" economics.

It is easy enough in these terms to explain why Louisiana lagged in the early 1970s. In 1957 state and local tax revenue collected just about 13 percent of state personal income, by far the highest tax burden in the Southeast. (We define tax burden consistently as state and local tax revenue as a percentage of state personal income.) This tax burden even exceeded the national average. Louisiana's tax history has been unique in the South, the result of the politics of Huey and Earl Long. Huey shattered the political patterns of post-Reconstruction Louisiana by pushing through increased

---

19. Louisiana Association of Business and Industry, "The Un-Stalled Louisiana Economy" (July 1981).

government spending and taxation. His brother went even further. From 1948 to 1952 Governor Earl Long drastically increased welfare spending, raised the education outlay to the national average (a startling act in a southern state), and boosted taxes by 50 percent. By 1952 Louisiana's state and local tax burden was the highest in the country. Even under a conservative Republican governor, Louisiana today takes every optional Medicaid program.[20]

Static tax levels alone, however, do not fully explain the state's economic performance. Even during the mid-1970 turnaround, the state's tax burden remained the region's highest. In its most widely circulated form this static figure masks several crucial developments. First of all, the state draws a uniquely high proportion of its budget from severance taxes. Theory and evidence suggest that these taxes on natural resources do not impose an economic burden at all similar to that of the more standard personal or business taxes. In Figure 1, we adjust the tax burden figures to remove the misleading impact of severance taxes.[21] The state tax burden remains high in the early 1970s compared to the Sunbelt, but not nearly as high as it was compared to the nation. Second, and even more important, Figure 1 shows the *changes* in the state tax burden. Taking the burden as a proportion of the average for all fifty states, we can see that it fell in the 1960s—an earlier period of state growth—turned upward in the early 1970s—a surge followed by the economic stall—and then began dropping sharply in 1974. This last decline can be attributed to the new state constitution approved by voters on April 20, 1974.

In a sense Louisiana was the first sequel to California's 1970 debate on

20. ACIR, *Significant Features of Fiscal Federalism*, 1979–80 ed. (Washington, D. C.: ACIR, October 1980), table 35, pp. 46–47; Allan P. Sindler, *Huey Long's Louisiana: State Politics, 1920–1952* (Baltimore: Johns Hopkins University Press, 1956), pp. 208–209; Thomas R. Beard, ed., *The Louisiana Economy* (Baton Rouge: Louisiana State University Press, 1969), pp. 197–200.

21. Arbitrarily assuming that 20 percent of the severance tax burden was felt within the state, we subtracted 80 percent of total severance tax receipts from total state and local tax revenues, and used the result in calculating state tax burden and state tax burden as a proportion of the national average.

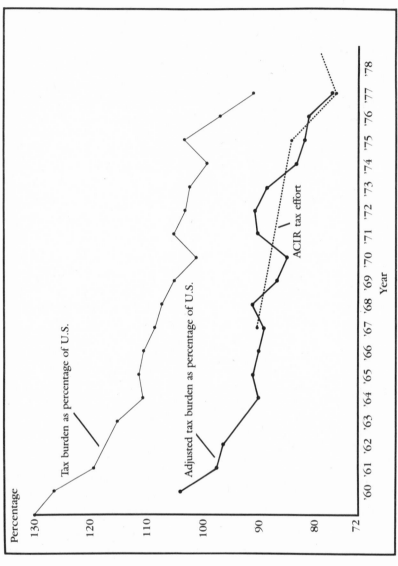

Figure 1. Changes in the Louisiana state tax burden, 1960–1980.

Proposition One, the opening shot of the tax revolt of the 1970s. Voters in California narrowly rejected that proposal, which ironically was far more limited than the tax and spending initiatives that they passed at the end of the decade. But conservatives and populists in Louisiana decided to repeat the experiment. One strain of thought in the 1973 constitutional convention, led by state representative Louis ("Woody") Jenkins, proposed a spending limit modelled on Proposition One. (This limit was later passed as a statute.) But the convention followed the populist lead of Jefferson Parish Assessor Lawrence A. Chehardy and adopted a series of specific tax restrictions.[22] When the new constitution took effect on December 31, 1974, it continued the previous constitution's freeze on personal income tax rates, allowed deduction of federal income taxes, prohibited local income taxes, set a ceiling on local sales taxes, and expanded the homestead exemption to the point that 97 percent of all homes escaped property taxation.[23] This policy has been a mixed blessing. The local revenue limits have placed New Orleans in a kind of fiscal trap similar to that of Boston in Massachusetts. Although tax reductions in both states have fostered a booming economy, the major cities have been denied a tax structure that allows them to tap that growth. As a result they are running out of money while facing increased demands on services and capital plant.

Furthermore, there are a number of other theses for Louisiana's growth. There may be a spillover from increasingly congested Texas; OPEC price increases have vastly increased the value of oil and gas production; and the natural gas discoveries in the "Tuscaloosa Trend" are generating fabulous wealth. These points are all true, yet our emphasis on tax burdens is not simply arbitrary. The Louisiana case fits a growing body of empirical evidence that illuminates the theory of what is called supply-side economics.

One of the first to signal the importance of changing tax burdens was economist Bernard L. Weinstein, who in migrating from New York State

22. Interviews with State Representative Jenkins, Lawrence A. Chehardy, and Lawrence E. Chehardy.

23. Louisiana Public Affairs Research Council, *PAR's Voter's Guide to the 1974 Proposed Constitution* (Baton Rouge: PAR, 1974), pp. 27–28.

to Texas had seen firsthand the impact at both ends of the curve.[24] But his published data covered too broad a period and averaged together periods of significantly different economic behavior, so he gave this factor less weight than it deserves. More sophisticated methods assign it even greater importance. Since no state or pairing of states can give us a completely unambiguous economic laboratory, the favored method of showing a connection between economic growth and its possible causes is to compare the experience of all fifty states through a statistical method called "regression analysis." In November 1978 two economists at Chicago's Harris Bank, Robert J. Genetski and Young D. Chin, published a fascinating first attempt to measure the economic impact of the "tax revolt."[25] They started with a state's economic growth in relation to the average U. S. performance (using personal income growth as the proxy). Working with data from 1969 to 1976, they found no relation to a state's static average tax burden (including all state and local taxes). But when they measured the *change* in state tax burden, a loose relation began to emerge. And when they allowed a three-year lag, to give a changing tax burden time to affect economic decisions, they found that they had discovered an "extremely strong" relationship. "For every 1 percent increase in a state's relative tax burden growth over the period analysed," they concluded, "growth declines by approximately 1/2 percent and vice versa."

This effort was admittedly crude, and there have been half-hearted attempts to discredit it. Yet it provides a striking confirmation of the theory popularized as the "Laffer Curve." Professor Arthur Laffer argues that beyond a certain optimum point, tax rates become counterproductive. They displace production into less efficient activity, such as tax shelters, or discourage people from working altogether. In such circumstances, the road to economic revival (and hence a healthier tax base) lies through reducing

24. Bernard L. Weinstein and Robert E. Firestine, *Regional Growth and Decline in the United States: The Rise of the Sunbelt and the Decline of the Northeast* (New York: Praeger Publishers, 1978), pp. 139–43.

25. Robert J. Genetski and Young D. Chin, "The Impact of State and Local Taxes on Economic Growth" (Harris Economic Research Office Service, November 3, 1978; available from Harris Trust and Savings Bank, Chicago, Illinois).

tax rates. The Genetski-Chin study is particularly striking because it forces us to elaborate this theory in a way that, although unexpected, turns out to be entirely consistent with the most profound observations of human behavior. The crucial decisions on producing or not producing, staying put or relocating, come not because a tax burden is high in absolute terms, but because it is changing. A pattern of increases, and the expectation of more, becomes a powerful discouragement. A pattern of decreases unleashes pent-up energies. The pattern is more than reminiscent of Tocqueville's observation that revolutions occur not when things are absolutely bad, but when they are changing, for either the worse or the better.[26]

The Genetski Regression thus gives us one powerful explanation for the early 1970s surge of the Sunbelt. According to the ACIR figures, during the decade 1965 to 1975 the annual average increase in tax burden in the Southwest was a full percentage point below the national average. And it explains the recent exceptional performance of Louisiana. In the last half of the 1970s only Louisiana, of the southeastern states, has fallen as much as one percentage point below the national average. And this tax burden decline is even more dramatic when we adjust for severance taxes.

We must add one more epicycle to this argument. Some of the studies following Genetski have confirmed the importance of the tax factor in the 1970s. Yet they find no statistically significant correlation for the 1960s.[27] The explanation is simple. State and local tax burdens are a small fraction of the federal tax burden. Their impact is further diluted by the fact that they can be deducted from federal returns. If federal tax rates are near the optimum point on the Laffer Curve, or descending the curve, as they were with the Kennedy tax cuts, the impact of state tax differences will be negligible. As the federal tax burden increases, however, the marginal difference of state tax burden becomes much more important. The sharp increase in

26. The phenomenon is also compatible with the thesis of Ted Robert Gurr in *Why Men Rebel* (Princeton: Princeton University Press, 1970), an attempt to derive a theory of political violence.

27. David S. Dahl and Samuel H. Gane, "The Impact of State and Local Taxes on Economic Growth" (Research Department, Federal Reserve Bank of Minneapolis, Working Paper No. 129, May 1979).

federal tax burdens cannot be denied. It is no theoretical problem that the Genetski Regression varies in different periods. In fact, this fluctuation could conceivably become a statistical tool for measuring the extent to which the federal tax burden exceeds the optimum point of the Laffer Curve.

To the extent that the federal tax burden increases, economic prospects look bright for those states with declining tax burdens. Yet nothing dictates that these states will be located in what is geographically called the Sunbelt. In fact prospects look most promising for two kinds of states: those that draw a large percentage of their revenue from severance taxes (which, as we have noted, do not seem to impose the same sort of economic burden that personal and business taxes do) and those that are reversing a pattern of excessive taxation. From 1978 to 1980 the most dramatic tax burden reduction in the country occurred in California, and its economy responded accordingly. Tax reductions in Massachusetts coincide with a high-technology boom. Its decaying mill towns now have among the lowest unemployment rates in the country. Even New York has arrested its economic collapse. As with so many media fads, just as the Sunbelt-Frostbelt conflict became a staple of the daily press, it was being superseded by a new economic reality. The Sunbelt, then, may not necessarily be "southern."

This conclusion may seem awkward in a collection of essays devoted to southern identity. Yet there are strands in southern history that may have predisposed the region to pursue a strategy of lowered taxes and to derive benefits when the federal tax burden pushed the state tax differential into prominence. Underneath the technical jargon, the debate over the Laffer Curve is really the ancient argument over whether money is more wisely spent by the government or the citizen in a free market. Critics of Professor Laffer and the "supply-siders" maintain that tax cuts would weaken the economy, because they would prevent the government from investing in needed infrastructure. This argument is somewhat harder to maintain when the bulk of federal domestic spending goes into transfer payments such as Social Security and welfare, and state budgets in the last decade have evolved in the same direction. The South has gone through one formative experience that makes it wary of this argument, namely Reconstruction.

It would be foolish to stray far from the racial issue in Reconstruction, yet this period has a fascinating economic and fiscal side. The Reconstruction governments in the South have been interpreted as some of the earliest and most massive welfare state experiments in American history. They launched expensive social programs supported by high rates of taxation or at least expanded state services far beyond their antebellum level. The experience made a great impression on the property owners and entrepreneurs who eventually wrested back control of state government, and tax reductions figured large in their agenda. This fiscal subplot is entirely overshadowed by questions of race and reaction, yet a series of southern states toward the end of Reconstruction staged what can be called an unalloyed form of tax revolt. In Texas, the Tax Payer's Convention movement attracted the support of disaffected Radical Republicans and went to some lengths to disassociate itself from racial issues. The post–Civil War period was one of sharply rising tax burdens, in the North as well as the South, and the state fiscal history of those years deserves fresh study of the sort that we have been attempting to give to the Sunbelt.[28]

The purpose of this essay, after all, has been to locate some general principle to explain the economic phenomenon of the Sunbelt, and to explain it not only when it holds together, but when it falls apart. If we are successful, we should be able to illuminate not only specific case studies like Louisiana but also a broad range of developments, north and south, late nineteenth or late twentieth century. State fiscal and economic history is too diverse to reduce always and in every detail to a single explanation. But the impact of rising and falling tax burdens has made enough of a difference in a wide enough variety of circumstances to warrant serious attention. At the very least, it should exert some discipline on overfacile generalizations about regional success or failure.

28. For a more detailed account, see James R. Adams, *The Secret History of the Tax Revolt* (work in progress).

☆ ☆ ☆ **10** ☆ ☆ ☆

Thoughts on the Dixiefication of Dixie

EDWIN M. YODER, JR.

. . . mute speculation, the patient curse
That stones the eyes, or like the jaguar leaps
For his own image in a jungle pool,
his victim.

—Allen Tate, "Ode to the Confederate Dead"

I sometimes think with amazement how little my own children, who are of the modern suburban South, know of the region that existed only a few decades ago. If I told them about it—and if they listened, as I once listened to the family storytellers—they would surely think my South as strange and exotic as Xanadu. No sacred rivers ran through it (unless the Suwannee), and there were no measureless caverns. What was exotic about it was a texture of human experience now vanished.

It was, for those of us who were fortunate, a cozy and settled place of black servitude (to call it by its right name) and white paternalism, often generous and gentle but insensitive. That South, once so familiar to some of us over the age of forty, was probably closer in feature and spirit to the South of a century earlier than it would be to the present South. With the barest jog of memory, one can recall the rattle of mule-drawn wagons in which people came to plow the garden, unhitching the animal for the job, or returned the gleaming wicker basket of linens sent out the week before to be stewed, no doubt, in a distant iron pot in the country. One recalls the cry of street vendors in an old town on the Savannah River, melodically touting blackberries and garden vegetables still wet with dew; the early-morning whistle of the men who mowed and raked the yard; the next-door maid with the voice of operatic volume making the summer air ring with spirituals; the Georgia cousins mischievously teasing cooks in the kitchen about the razor blades that they allegedly hid in the folds of their stockings; the fetishes about doors and drinking glasses. It almost seems a caricature now.

This was, of course, a physical South—a South of props and roles dutifully played even by those who must have sensed in them the fragility of the theatrical. Anyway, the sets are long since stored and the script much revised. So the South that journalists, professors, and critics now tend to discuss at symposia—speaking, usually, as keepers of the flame—is not the experienced South but the South of memory and imagination, sometimes not less real. It is the South made present to us by Flannery O'Connor, Erskine Caldwell, Eudora Welty, and William Faulkner: a region of Tobacco Road and Yoknapatawpha. It is also the historical South of C. Vann Woodward and David Potter, the South portrayed or deduced from its past. All these Souths exist by a determined act of will, evocation, and self-consciousness. It is the South conceptualized, the flesh made word, the South that replenishes itself as, one by one, the solid stage props wear out.

It would be a daring student of that South who would say that it is finished. Yet few would, I think, deny that there is a certain burden and exertion in keeping it alive. I confess, in my own case, to a certain fatigue with this South of the imagination, in its more ghostly and disembodied forms. After seven years of absence from the region I find that my perspective has shifted in subtle ways. I still believe in *southerners*, for whose existence the evidence continues to be very real. But to believe in the larger abstraction called "the South" requires an increasing ingenuity and energy. The symposia continue. But how long has it been since we heard something genuinely novel said about the South or the southern experience?

As I review the influences that shaped my own regional consciousness—and of course all of us were southerners a long time before we began to think about it, as M. Jourdain had spoken prose a long time before he was told what it was—certain formative events stand out, events for which I find no recent parallels. The first, for me, after discovering W. J. Cash's *The Mind of the South* as a college sophomore (a fateful age to do so), was foreign travel, distancing the experience of growing up southern and suggesting that the assimilationist pressures of "Americanism" then (the early and mid-1950s) so much in the air might be eccentric to the larger world's experience: a point soon to be memorably made by C. Vann Woodward. In fact, the publication in 1959 of *The Burden of Southern History*, with its central essay "The Search for Southern Identity," was far the most important event for me after the Cash revival. Woodward's essays quickly became and remained a touchstone for defining (or refining) one's regional imagination. Like a mineral trace they run in our blood and marrow now, carrying the notion that the southern experience of history had been touched with distinctiveness and was rather *un*American when it came to the point: that it involved guilt, not innocence; pessimism, not optimism; the experience of social tragedy and intractability, not easy progress; defeat, not victory; poverty, not riches. All of this made impressive sense to me at the time. The marks of it remain as indelible as the marks of Faulkner's great novels. The time and setting, moreover, were just right. The late 1950s and early 1960s—when so much of national importance was happening in and to the South—assured a cresting of interest in what it was like to be southern. We southerners were studied hard, everywhere, like savages brought in from a newly discovered continent in the Elizabethan Age.

Now, twenty years later, I sense that all this has changed. Where before there was a feeling that the South, guided through travail by its tragic bards to some deeper sense of guilt and gallantry, might become a fascinating showpiece of national destiny, there is now, I sense, a mood of boredom and impatience. As a theme for defining the national experience, regionalism has yielded to ethnicity. But despite some ingenious writing on the southerner-as-ethnic, it is not obvious what it adds to one's self-identification to imagine oneself a Pole or an Irishman with a difference.

Symptomatic, I believe, of this impatience was an amusing magazine article published four years ago by Norman Podhoretz, editor of *Commentary:* "How the North Was Won." Once a patron and publisher of literary southerners, Mr. Podhoretz is now weary of a style that he views in retrospect as deplorably subversive of Yankee character. He pictures for us an invasion of New York by cadres of southern literati: a small company of white southerners who intrigued their way into the editorial chairs of influential national magazines of the sixties, soon plunging the poor North into frenzies of racial guilt before it quite knew what was going on. The secret weapon of these neo-Confederate agents was the charm of their pens. They were, Mr. Podhoretz suggests, children of guilt atoned, compensating at the typewriter for the down-home bigotries that they grew up with. Worst of all, they identified the traditional ethnic enclaves of New York City (and other places) as ghettos, portraying an expression of affinity as an expression of racism. "The North," writes Mr. Podhoretz, "had no chance against the ascendant Southerly analysis of those realities, with its simplistic diagnosis of racism as the prime cause of all the black man's woes."[1]

I am less concerned here with analyzing this ingenious but fallacious theory than with noting its importance as a symptom. For surely it signaled the end of a submissive fascination with southern regionalism by our sometime collaborators among the New York ethnic intelligentsia. Not the least of Mr. Podhoretz's complaints, significantly, is that this southern literary coup heralded and foreshadowed the later election of James Earl Carter as president, with its populist tone and, as Mr. Podhoretz sees it, its scorn of middle-class urban values. No one is very happy today with that experience, although our own unhappiness must necessarily differ from Norman Podhoretz's. Mr. Carter was, after all, the first authentic southerner to become president in more than a century. Bearing Woodward's thesis in mind, we might have expected him to exhibit that sense of historical complexity and tragedy that the historian found to be close to the core of the

---

1. Norman Podhoretz, "How the North Was Won," *New York Times Magazine* (September 30, 1979): 63.

southern experience. But the appearance, at least, was often to the contrary. So far as a sense of history was concerned, Mr. Carter traveled light.[2] It was not so much a sense of tragedy as of rationalism, optimism, excessive deference to popular vanity, the engineer's illusion of a manipulable world, that became the hallmarks of the Carter style. His claim to be a student of Reinhold Niebuhr, hence presumably a sort of historical pessimist, did not sustain exacting scrutiny. That recent foreign-policy failures reflected a larger failure to tap the innate "goodness" of people in the mass— one of Mr. Carter's early themes—was about the last thing one could imagine Niebuhr suggesting. Having ventured, as other southerners did, to hope that we could expect a subsidence of facile secularism and moralism under Mr. Carter, I was as disappointed as Mr. Podhoretz, though for very different reasons.

The Carter experience (and I am offering here no sweeping judgment on his presidency, especially by comparison with the simplicities of judgment and optimism that now seem to have come after it) suggests, for one thing, the limits of the Woodward thesis. Indeed, it gives life to Richard King's suggestion that the insights provided by essays like "The Search for Southern Identity" are of more instructive than descriptive value. "The central problem with Woodward's eloquent essay," writes Richard King in *A Southern Renaissance*, "was that it was difficult to detect which southerners gave evidence of having learned from the region's unhappy history or at

2. See James Fallows, "The Passionless Preidency," *Atlantic Monthly* (May 1979): 33–48. Fallows, Mr. Carter's chief speechwriter, offers several interesting comments on the president's sense of history, e.g.: "It often seemed to me that 'history' for Carter and those closest to him, consisted of Vietnam and Watergate; if they could avoid the errors, as commonly understood, of those two episodes, they would score well. No military intervention, no dirty tricks, no tape recorders on the premises, and no 'isolation' of the president" (p. 38). "The first clue. . . was Carter's cast of mind: his view of problems as technical, not historical, his lack of curiosity about how the story turned out before. . . . In two years, the only historical allusions I heard Carter use with any frequency were Harry Truman's rise from the depths of the polls and the effect of Roosevelt's New Deal on the southern farm. . . . Carter occasionally read history—he loved David McCollough's book on the Panama Canal—but history had not become a part of him. . . . Later I read that he had decided that history was important, and that he needed a better background for his job" (pp. 44–45).

least of having learned what Woodward wanted them to learn. In this sense Woodward's essay was addressed as much to the South as it was to the rest of the nation, and expressed a hope for what Southerners might come to believe in the future as much as it described the present state of Southern historical consciousness."[3] However the case might be, Jimmy Carter had possibly missed the point either way. One wondered, with King, how many other southerners had missed it also.

It was perhaps unreasonable to expect that the first southern president in a century or more would know, or school the nation in, those hard historical lessons of our imagining. The presidency remains a bully pulpit, but Carter found other matters to preach upon. Nor, perhaps, should we make too much of Norman Podhoretz's disillusionment with the "southerly analysis," since he is troubled about many things these days. But Mr. Carter's failure to act up to the historical role that we as southerners might have coveted for him, and the fatigue registered by Mr. Podhoretz, echo a certain impatience with southern myth, inside and outside the family.

This would not necessarily concern us, who deem it our role to keep the flame of regionalism alive, if we could be confident that our myths and preoccupations were grounded in a solid social reality. Are they? Might we be approaching a time when the southernizing enterprise flirts with obscurantism and self-caricature? When might it become a matter of, if you will, Dixiefying Dixie: putting a sort of stage-prop front on a mercurial reality? This has been, for southern intellectuals, a lurking worry all along.

In a piece I wrote for Willie Morris in 1964 about W. J. Cash, I spoke of "the tacit alliance that reaches down from the rarified meditations of professors, authors, and journalists to the inchoate consciousness of the leather-jacketed hot-rodder who sports a Confederate flag on the rear bumper." There was, I suggested, "little doubt that if the South lacked working mythologists to go on holding up a mirror to 'the mind of the South' this mind would vanish as a distinctive study in self-consciousness."[4] I was still disconcerted by the possibility even some years later

3. Richard King, *A Southern Renaissance: The Cultural Awakening of the American South, 1930–1955* (New York: Oxford University Press, 1980), p. 275.

4. "W. J. Cash After a Quarter Century," in Willie Morris, ed., *The South Today, 100 Years After Appomattox* (New York: Harper & Row, 1965), pp. 98, 99.

when I introduced John Shelton Reed's *The Enduring South* and admitted that in the dark of night those of us who traffic in southern "differences" contemplate our profession in terror: "Is [one] dealing in tomfoolery, or raising ancient spirits better left sleeping? Is [one] a cotton-patch Spengler, a Lysenko of the magnolia groves?"[5]

I assumed then that those questions were rhetorical and that negative answers might safely be expected. I still think so, but with less assurance. The continuing exercise in regional self-consciousness, when it is all that stands between "the South" and its disappearance, was assuredly worth the candle when we could plausibly suppose that a distinctive historical experience was at stake, when that experience had direct political consequences in a nation given to utopianism, or when the point was to repel facile cant about a national "mainstream" in which the South should, for its sins, immediately immerse itself. (Happily, as George B. Tindall has observed, "it is not the South that has vanished but the mainstream, like one of those desert rivers that run out into the sand, consumed by the heat."[6]) Our somewhat narcissistic enterprise could be indulged to constructive purpose so long as we were confident of a special sensibility, of a literature demonstrably richer and more searching than any other in America, and even when we could suggest with a straight face that our statecraft was something quite special.

But what now? What do we do when we begin to suspect that there may be more smoke than fire? Is it really for slick country music, or franchise fried chicken, or a resurgent Ku Klux Klan, or for grotesquely reactionary politicians that so much ink is spilled? Is the nourishing of these things, *faute de mieux*, not the essence of what I call Dixiefying Dixie? I know the pitfalls of all this, even as I write it. The South of imagination and memory has shown great tenacity in the face of physical, political, economic, social, and maybe even psychological change. But new times demand new themes. And the discovery of new themes might mean, incidentally, facing

5. "Foreword," in John Shelton Reed, *The Enduring South: Subcultural Persistence in Mass Society* (Lexington, Mass.: Lexington Books, 1972; reprint ed., Chapel Hill: University of North Carolina Press, 1974), p. xv.

6. George B. Tindall, "Beyond the Mainstream," in *The Ethnic Southerners* (Baton Rouge: Louisiana State University Press, 1976), p. 4.

up to our own ambivalence about change. Was it facile to believe, as some of us did as recently as ten or fifteen years ago, that what was good and valuable in southern custom, experience, myth, and manners could be preserved, while the dross of evil was slowly refined away? Was the dross actually consumed, or has it now merely reached its rococco stage?

Of course, even in our willingness to part with the South of memory and imagination, along with the physical South of which I spoke briefly at the outset, we would often be offended by the tawdriness of what was left. We might find ourselves exclaiming, with Ophelia, "O, what a falling-off was here!" and seeking mental refuge in a sullen sense that we had lived before the revolution and had known the gentleness of life. But even this sullen sense of loss might be preferable to a merely antiquarian regionalism, a fly-in-amber quaintness. I do not know, and would not venture to predict, whether it would or not. All I know is that *my* South is fading and that I find it difficult to muster the will or imagination to revive or restore it. Nonetheless I must close with the usual disclaimer. I would like to be shown to be another, neither the first nor yet perhaps the last, who prematurely consigned the South to the boneyard. Maybe Dixie can be Dixiefied yet again. It is a rash man who dismisses the possibility.

The South and the World
A Dissenting Postscript

HODDING CARTER

There is good reason to beware the person who appears under a banner as broad as mine. The topic, "The South and the World," leaves latitude for a multitude of sins, as well as subjects. It also presupposes a level of expertise about both the South and the world that I cannot honestly claim. There is equally good reason to beware of journalists in general, this volume and my presence notwithstanding. They can be skillful recorders and arrangers of facts. They may even be adequate analysts and interpreters. But they inevitably deal with raw material provided by others and rarely transform the material with enough vision in a time of rapid change. For that you need the creative chemistry of the novelist and poet, or poets of history such as C. Vann Woodward. There will be no such transubstantiation in what I offer here.

But no matter. We are partners in a shared venture across a turbulent and starkly uncharted sea. We have already come a great distance here at home, only to discover what a great distance remains ahead. We exist in a larger world almost wholly inaccessible to those enthralled by some of the most popular doctrines of old. Despite enduring attachments to this particular theory of cause and effect, only two groups of people still profess to believe that events can be explained by reference to the international Communist conspiracy. One is composed of the aging totalitarians who preside over their decaying empire behind the Kremlin's walls. The other is made up of those within our loosely defined "free world" who are emotionally and intellectually incapable of distinguishing between the imperatives of the Bill of Rights and the theories of the Communist Manifesto, especially in times of turbulence.

Against this background, let us examine our past and prospects together. We shall do so as members of a human race largely populated by the nonwhite, the poor, and the repressed. It is a population whose description would have done for a shorthand version of the South's a century ago. That it no longer fits the South is the result of a revolution—a word that terrifies many white southerners and Americans generally, but a fact that dramatically altered the societal landscape of our region within the past generation.

Karl Marx once said of the southern Confederacy, "It is not a country at all, but a battle slogan." Ulrich B. Phillips, historian and avid champion of white supremacy, could accurately observe that the South found its unity in "a common resolve indomitably maintained—that it shall be and remain a white man's country." That, he wrote, is "the cardinal test of a Southerner and the central theme of Southern history."[1] My children would find that definition of the South ludicrous, even if they encountered it in their daily lives. They do not.

It was not ludicrous for most of us just yesterday. When James Silver titled his landmark book, *Mississippi: The Closed Society*, he won the truth-in-packaging award for the entire decade of the 1960s, and indeed for all the decades stretching forward from the Civil War. Deadening conformity to "our way of life" was demanded and enforced. It took courage for a black man and a white man to shake hands in public back in 1959, the year I returned to my home town of Greenville, Mississippi. It was worth a black man's life for him to venture such a familiarity with a white woman. It was almost equally foolhardy to advocate an end to segregation, whether political, economic, or social. The white dissenter was easily isolated in our

---

1. Ulrich B. Phillips, "The Central Theme of Southern History," *American Historical Review* 34 (October 1928): 31.

heavily rural society; the black dissenter was all too readily eliminated. Blacks tried to vote at risk of injury or death in much of the South, went to schools so inferior as to be outside the parameters of real education, and worked virtually without exception at jobs considered too menial for whites.

We were obsessed with race. I don't remember a day in the years between 1959 and 1972 when I didn't think about it, worry about it, and respond to it. Race defined the important meets and bounds of our existence. That curse is gone. Ulrich Phillips's "cardinal test" is no longer applied. It is no longer necessary for a white politician to cry "nigger, nigger" to be elected. Black southerners have been freed somewhat. White southerners have been almost totally liberated, if they are willing to use their freedom.

Our schools are the most integrated in the nation, rather than the most segregated. There are more black elected officials in the South than in any other region. Some of our greatest cities, from Atlanta to Birmingham to New Orleans, have black mayors. A white southerner, the boulder of legally mandated racism lifted from his path, was elected president on the strength of regional solidarity, black and white, then dumped in a national landslide in which the South fully participated. Regional pride was no match for the nearly universal perception that he lacked the focus, commitment, and strength that the job requires. Perhaps most notably in a society where caste is heavily determined by money, economic deprivation has diminished substantially for most whites and some blacks. The road seems to be moving up, rather than down.

If we left it there, it would sound like the great American success story, courage and morality conquering all. But we all know that it isn't the whole story. We reached the moral plateau that the nation once demanded of us in race relations and discovered just how low it always was. We have barely begun to meet the demands that a just society must impose on itself. We created shining cities like Atlanta and Houston, and left behind a thousand small towns and rural counties—communities of deep, endemic poverty and no apparent hope of change. We embraced the American dream, translated into sprawling suburbia, freeways, and urban anonymity, and wonder why it leaves us so dissatisfied with the texture of our lives—in those moments when we abandon the modern hustle long enough to reflect.

Some of us ventured into a new politics, then discovered that government is a limited instrument for creating community and a poor one for dealing with some of our most basic needs. While we weren't looking, or were smugly pretending that the New South had finally dawned, the old politics reasserted itself in a new guise. We no longer think about race all the time, but we know nonetheless that the reality of race will not go away. No longer segregated by law, we remain segregated in fact most of our daily lives. Despite occasionally fanciful rhetoric to the contrary, most of it from nonsoutherners or expatriate southerners, we are not forging a new, closer relationship between black and white. We are still a region of strangers, despite the truth that we are more intimately bound together in the South than elsewhere in the country.

A determinist of the narrowest sort might leave it there. For me, at least, what is exciting about the South today is that there is no convincing reason to say that it is fated to go one way or another. Our history is no longer our future, because to a meaningful extent we are free of it for the first time. Indeed, history now offers us an opportunity and a challenge, but it is moving rapidly. Crossroads are being reached and passed without sufficient attention to the roads not taken.

If the South has been radically transformed over the past twenty years, so too has the world beyond our borders. If the future remains to be written in the South, so too is it at issue among the more than four billion human beings who are not Americans. If the problems that lie in our path are staggering, those that lie in the way of most of mankind seem almost without solution.

Having, as Sheldon Hackney has written, a southern "feeling of persecution at times and a sense of being a passive, insignificant object of alien or impersonal forces," that reaction in others should be no surprise. As Woodward put it in a different context, the South has never been able to share the North's certainty that "history is something unpleasant that happens to other people." Thus, having also been American "a long time be-

fore [he] was Southern in any self-conscious or distinctive way," the southerner "should be secure enough in his national identity to escape the
compulsion of less secure minorities to embrace uncritically all the myths
of nationalism." To all of which I must add, sadly but firmly, my dissenting
postscript. That which might be is not that which is. The South that produced the nation's first secretary of state, Thomas Jefferson, and then its
greatest and most visionary, George C. Marshall, is the South that remains
unyieldingly chauvinistic in its approach to the rest of the world.

First in war; that most certainly. We do not lack for patriots and heroes,
for which we can rightly be proud. But in peace, our record in the world is
increasingly a narrow and unhappy one, a reversion to the day when
southern freebooters assaulting the Caribbean gave American meaning to
the word "filibuster." Politicians of broad vision represented us not long
ago. William Fulbright of Arkansas, Albert Gore of Tennessee, Frank
Graham of North Carolina, and John Sparkman of Alabama spoke and
voted for our active partnership and compassionate commitment in a
world that desperately needed both. Some still echo and reinforce their
themes, but far fewer than before. The martial refrain, always insistent in
southern history, swells and drowns out the internationalist. The free
traders, the Cordell Hulls and Will Claytons, have been replaced by narrow protectionists intent on closing American markets to foreign commerce. Southern politicians look out at a world of dizzying change and
profess to see the Red hand behind each upheaval, much as their predeces-
sors once claimed that Communists were responsible for the civil rights
movement. As a region, we find it easy to endorse the garrison state approach as a solution to the world's complexities.

Let me identify my own position. It is vital that the United States be
militarily strong, as strong as any opponent. It is essential that we recognize and never forget that the Soviet Union, by ideology and by habit,
does and will exploit every available opportunity for mischief and control.
Sweet reason and an open checkbook will not suffice as counters to its
drive. But we, above all other Americans, should know how irrelevant the
desires of Moscow and Washington are to the bedrock concerns and pas-
sions of most people in the world. If neither capital existed, Israelis and

Arabs would still be locked in mortal combat; Protestants and Catholics would be killing each other in Ireland, just as they did long before Karl Marx or Adam Smith; black majorities would still be seeking an end to white minority rule in South Africa; Chinese and Indochinese would be disputing territory and regional hegemony, as they have for centuries; Iranian and Iraqi would be at each other's throats; those held under the boot, whatever the nature of the regime, would be seeking to destroy it; and those controlling essential resources would be demanding top dollar for their sale.

We southerners, too, should understand how deadening is any policy that is negative rather than positive. Having been through a revolution based on the demand for human rights, we should know that the most powerful force in the world, except for survival itself, is the idea of freedom and individual dignity. To stand forth in favor of that idea is to stand forth in favor of our fundamental principles; to abandon it is to betray ourselves, just as America betrayed itself with legally mandated segregation. We prickly sticklers for regional and states' rights should be able to understand that no nation that respects itself is going to do the unquestioned will of another, unless its subservience is purchased or imposed. Finally, we should have enough sense of history to know that there is no quick fix and no final solution. History happens to us, and history goes on. What is required is the will to engage and the patience to stay a very long course. In that, white Americans could learn something from black Americans, who refused to give up in a nation that first held them as slaves, then treated them as serfs, and only lately has begun slowly to allow them to participate as full citizens.

Let me conclude with some shameless, though duly acknowledged, plagiarization. In 1940, W. J. Cash ended *The Mind of the South* with the following words:

> In the coming days, and probably soon, [the South] is likely to have to prove its capacity for adjustment far beyond what has been true in the past. And in the time I shall hope, as its loyal son, that its virtues will tower over and conquer its faults and have the making

of the Southern world to come. But of the future I shall venture no definite prophecies. It would be a brave man who would venture them in any case. It would be a madman who would venture them in the face of forces sweeping over the world in the fateful year of 1940.[2]

To which, amen for 1983.

Then there are the words of Charles Longstreet Weltner, former congressman from Atlanta, in his 1966 autobiography, *Southerner:*

> We are not hopelessly condemned to relive history. Rather, if we have the wit and the will, we can add a new and brighter chapter to Southern history. Our fundamental charter declares all men created equal. Our basic religion declares us our brother's keeper. But the demand for justice rests not alone on legal precept or theological tenet. It is a demand that spans creed and clan, age and continent. It speaks now as it has to prophet, saint, and patriot—and to unnumbered millions of men and women throughout all time. It wells from the heart as plain truth and clear duty. Let right be done.[3]

To which, amen and amen, for the South, for the nation, and for the world.

2. W. J. Cash, *The Mind of the South* (New York: Alfred A. Knopf, 1941, 1957).

3. Charles Longstreet Weltner, *Southerner* (Philadelphia: J. B. Lippincott Co., 1966), p. 188.

In Search of the Dixie Difference
A Guide to the Literature

JOHN B. BOLES

For decades historians, journalists, and social commentators have been searching for a definitive way to characterize the essence of the South. No one yet has been completely successful, but the collective effort has produced an intriguing subgenre of southern literature. Even antebellum travelers attempted to explain both the observed and the imagined differences between the South and the rest of the nation, and none has been more influential than Frederick Law Olmsted. The best modern edition of his classic *The Cotton Kingdom* has recently been reprinted (New York: Alfred A. Knopf, 1983) with a perceptive new introduction by Lawrence N. Powell.

Ulrich B. Phillips, the Georgian who taught for years at Yale University, wrote over a half century ago one of the most important thumbnail characterizations of the southern past, "The Central Theme of Southern History," *American Historical Review* 34 (October 1928): 30–43. His emphasis on race as the defining issue for southerners has been much revised of late, but every discussion of the nature of southernness starts with his interpretation. During the 1920s a group of intellectuals centered at Vanderbilt University began to emphasize the South's agrarian past (part reality, part tragedy, part myth) as the region's identifying feature, and in a famous manifesto published in 1930 as *I'll Take My Stand* (New York: Harper &

Brothers), these "Twelve Southerners" exhorted their fellow southerners not to let Dixie become like the rest of America. A still more probing analysis of the region's history and character came a decade later from a North Carolinian, Wilbur J. Cash. Journalist Cash's tour de force, *The Mind of the South* (New York: Alfred A. Knopf, 1941), brilliantly written and argued, remains today as enthralling as it did forty years ago, though defending or attacking his provocative explication of the southern experience has become a cottage industry among historians.

During the late 1940s and early 1950s the nation had preoccupations other than the South, and except for Hodding Carter's *Southern Legacy* (Baton Rouge: Louisiana State University Press, 1950), most essayists addressed other issues. Then with the 1954 Supreme Court decision outlawing segregation, the nation's eyes turned again to the South, its peculiar traditions and its persisting heritage. *Arkansas Gazette* editor Harry S. Ashmore believed—hoped—that the South's basic nature was changing, and his *An Epitaph for Dixie* (New York: W. W. Norton & Company, 1958) suggested that the distinctiveness of the region was being destroyed by the forces of progress. Francis B. Simkins hoped otherwise, and a half decade later answered Ashmore's analysis with an eloquent defense of traditional Dixie, *The Everlasting South* (Baton Rouge: Louisiana State University Press, 1963).

Suddenly the nature of the South, its history and its people, became a pertinent topic. Charles G. Sellers edited a book of lively essays, *The Southerner as American* (Chapel Hill: University of North Carolina Press, 1960), that integrated the South into the American experience. David M. Potter followed with a classic essay, "The Enigma of the South," *Yale Review* 51 (Autumn 1961): 142–51, that examined the South as a folk culture. That same year William R. Taylor in *Cavalier and Yankee: The Old South and American National Character* (New York: George Braziller, Inc., 1961) probed the self-serving myths that both regions had about the other and themselves. Frank E. Vandiver edited a book of essays originally presented at Rice University, *The Idea of the South* (Chicago: University of Chicago Press, 1964), and two essays in the collection have been especially influential: Vandiver's own "The Southerner as Extremist" and George B. Tindall's "Mythology: A New Frontier in Southern History."

Howard Zinn argued in *The Southern Mystique* (New York: Alfred A. Knopf, 1964) that the alleged peculiarities of the South were only distortions and exaggerations of American folkways, perhaps a perverse way of suggesting that southerners were Americans after all. The April 1965 issue of *Harper's Magazine*, commemorating the centennial of Lee's surrender at Appomattox, featured a series of essays on the South. Those essays, revised and expanded, were issued in book form as *The South Today*, edited by Willie Morris (New York: Harper & Row, 1965). In his foreword Morris observed that the South was "the most written about area of America . . . ; it is perpetually ending or coming into its own, with a character that oscillates from doom to mere eccentricity" (p. vii). But the most important book on the nature of the South published in the 1960s suggested that it was the southern historical experience itself that set the South apart from the North. That book, of course, was C. Vann Woodward's collection of masterful essays, *The Burden of Southern History* (Baton Rouge: Louisiana State University Press, 1960). According to Woodward, the South—unlike the rest of the nation—had known failure, poverty, and guilt. And that profound difference shaped the southern response to history.

The search for a central theme to southern history if anything gained momentum in the 1970s, when prosperity and urban growth seemed to bring North and South together. John Sheldon Reed, a sociologist, conducted a sophisticated analysis of three decades of public opinion polls and discovered that while southern opinion had undergone a great change, so had that of the North, and the regions were as recognizably different in 1972 as they had been when Mr. Gallup began his surveys. Hence the title of Reed's book, *The Enduring South: Subcultural Persistence in Mass Society* (Lexington, Mass.: D. C. Heath and Company, 1972). Sheldon Hackney's incisive essay the following year, "The South as a Counterculture," *The American Scholar* 42 (Spring 1973): 283–93, corroborated Reed's findings.

The contributors to the colorfully titled *You Can't Eat Magnolias*, edited by H. Brandt Ayers and Thomas H. Naylor (New York: McGraw-Hill

Book Co., 1972), agreed that the South was a region set apart, but they called upon southerners to look beyond myths and racial stereotypes to see the problems that vexed the region. They urged the South to develop progressive policies aimed at solving southern afflictions in order to preserve what was good about the South's heritage. Less positive in tone was John Egerton's *The Americanization of Dixie: The Southernization of America* (New York: Harper & Row, 1974), who saw the two regions exchanging sins and achieving sectional rapprochement at the cost of the best within both subcultures.

In 1977 Carl N. Degler added an eloquent volume to the age-old debate over southern distinctiveness and the quarrel among historians over whether southern history had been marked more by change or continuity. His *Place Over Time: The Continuity of Southern Distinctiveness* (Baton Rouge: Louisiana State University Press) harked back to Phillips in his emphasis on race and to Potter in his emphasis on family, religion, and sense of place. George B. Tindall in *The Ethnic Southerners* (Baton Rouge: Louisiana State University Press, 1976), a collection of essays originally published between 1958 and 1976, found the roots of the persistence of southern distinctiveness to lie in the strong regional mythology. In different ways intellectual historians have probed this problem of cultural persistence (conservatism?) and the self-perception (myth?) of a distinctive South. Three outstanding recent analyses are: Michael O'Brien, *The Idea of the American South, 1920–1941* (Baltimore: Johns Hopkins University Press, 1979); Richard H. King, *A Southern Renaissance: The Cultural Awakening of the American South, 1930–1955* (New York: Oxford University Press, 1980); and Daniel J. Singal, *The War Within: From Victorian to Modernist Thought in the South, 1919–1945* (Chapel Hill: University of North Carolina Press, 1982).

"Fifteen Southerners" marked the fiftieth anniversary of the publication of *I'll Take My Stand* with another book of memorable essays, *Why the South Will Survive* (Athens, Ga.: University of Georgia Press, 1981). However, David R. Goldfield doubts that the familiar South of rural folkways and close family ties will survive; see his *Cotton Fields and Skyscrapers:*

Southern City and Region, 1607–1980 (Baton Rouge: Louisiana State University Press, 1982).

The *Journal of Southern History* has included many articles central to the search for southern distinctiveness and the origins and future of that distinctiveness. Two recent articles are particularly relevant: "The Northern Origins of Southern Mythology" by Patrick Gerster and Nicholas Cords, 43 (November 1977): 567–82; and "The Ever-Vanishing South," by Charles P. Roland, 48 (February 1982): 3–20. Forrest McDonald and Grady McWhiney have become identified in recent years with an ethnocultural interpretation of southern culture that emphasizes the Celtic origins of southern (white) civilization. The most complete elaboration of their position so far is "The South from Self-Sufficiency to Peonage: An Interpretation," *American Historical Review* 85 (December 1980): 1095–1111. According to their thesis, southerners like to fight, drink hard liquor, and avoid work (not labeled "laziness" but rather "the leisure ethic"). Perhaps this was the stereotype that William L. Miller had in mind when he entitled his study of Jimmy Carter *The Yankee from Georgia* (New York: Times Books, 1978).

The South is more than a geographical region with an identifiable ethos and folk, more than a historical concept; it occupies a significant niche in American literature and popular culture. Representative studies of the South in American literature are Louis D. Rubin, *The Faraway Country: Writers of the Modern South* (Seattle: University of Washington Press, 1963); F. Garvin Davenport, Jr., *The Myth of Southern History: Historical Consciousness in Twentieth-Century Southern Literature* (Nashville, Tenn.: Vanderbilt University Press, 1970); and Sylvia Jenkins Cook, *From Tobacco Road to Route 66: The Southern Poor White in Fiction* (Chapel Hill: University of North Carolina Press, 1976). The South in American popular culture has recently become an important subdivision of southern history. See Jack Temple Kirby, *Media-Made Dixie: The South in the American Imagination* (Baton Rouge: Louisiana State University Press, 1978); Bill C. Malone, *Southern Music/American Music* (Lexington, Ky.: University Press of Kentucky, 1979); Edward D. C. Campbell, *The Celluloid South: Hollywood and the Southern Myth* (Knoxville: University of Tennessee Press, 1981);

and the special issue of the *Journal of Popular Culture* 16 (Winter 1982), with an in-depth section entitled "The South and Popular Culture," pp. 1–96, consisting of nine articles edited by Christopher D. Geist.

It has become almost impossible to keep fully abreast of the scholarly literature on the South. Two historical journals focus exclusively on the region as a whole: *Southern Studies* and the *Journal of Southern History*. The latter journal, a quarterly, publishes articles and reviews of approximately 175 books annually, and in each May issue prints a detailed bibliography of scholarly periodical literature on southern history. For popular culture, one should consult such magazines as *Southern Living*.

Notes on Contributors

JAMES R. ADAMS

An editorial page writer for the *Wall Street Journal*, Mr. Adams recently
received his Ph.D. from Cornell University and is the author of a
forthcoming book, *The Secret History of the Tax Revolt*.

BRANDT AYERS

Editor and publisher of the *Anniston Star* in Alabama. Mr. Ayers was
co-editor ten years ago of another book of essays on the South,
You Can't Eat Magnolias.

JOHN B. BOLES

Professor of history at Rice University and managing editor of the
Journal of Southern History. He is the author of several books, including
Black Southerners, 1619–1869.

HODDING CARTER

Scion of an eminent Mississippi newspaper family and former assistant
secretary of state for public affairs in Jimmy Carter's administration.
Mr. Carter is now producer of the PBS television series, "Inside Story."

JOHN A. CROWL

Was editor and is now publisher of the *Chronicle of Higher Education*.

PAUL DELANEY

Deputy national editor of the *New York Times*.

WILMER C. FIELDS

Director of public relations of the Executive Committee of the Southern
Baptist Convention, and former editor of the Mississippi *Baptist Record*.

NEAL R. PEIRCE

A syndicated columnist specializing in state and urban affairs and a prolific author whose most recent work is the co-authored *The Book of America: Inside Fifty States Today*.

ROY REED

Now head of the Department of Journalism at the University of Arkansas, Mr. Reed was for years a reporter for the *New York Times* covering the Deep South out of New Orleans.

WILLIAM K. STEVENS

Acclimatized as the Houston bureau chief of the *New York Times*, he is now the New Delhi bureau chief.

W. L. TAITTE

Received his Ph.D. from Princeton University in English. Mr. Taitte is a contributing editor of *Texas Monthly* specializing in gourmet dining and high culture.

EDWIN M. YODER, JR.

A syndicated columnist and Rhodes Scholar who received a Pulitzer Prize for editorial writing with the *Washington Star*.